49er Irish

49er Irish

One Irish Family in the California Mines

F. D. Calhoon

AN EXPOSITION-LOCHINVAR BOOK

Exposition Press   *Hicksville, New York*

To Mike, a real hardrock miner

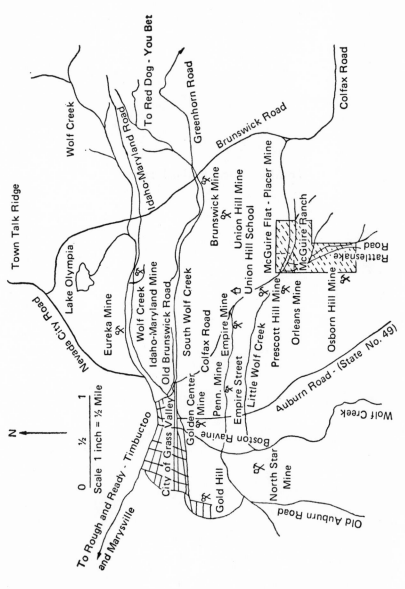

Taken from an old map of the Grass Valley mining district, made by Mike McGuire

Contents

THE McGUIRE FAMILY

Michael McGuire
1819-1908

Mary Cavanaugh
1829-1918
Children

Joseph (Joe)
1849-1918

Timothy (Tim)
1851-1875 (?)

Peter
1858-1873 (?)

Samuel (Sam)
1859-1873 (?)

Sarah (Mitchell)
1864-1933

Minnie (Shoemaker)
1866-1936

Thomas (Tom)
1872-1969

James (Jim)
1874-1946

Lucy (Rust)
1876-1956
Michael, Jr. (Mike)
1878-1964
Grandchildren

William Mitchell
Sister Celestine
Georgie Agnew
Alice Mourtier
Leah Grover
Carlos
Richard
Marian Calhoon
James

Prologue

Eric sat next to me on the chesterfield and gave me a big hug. That was entirely foreign to his nature. I reasoned correctly that I was about to have the "bite" put on me for something.

Eric is my eleven-year-old grandson. Like me, he is not overly demonstrative. I waited for the third out of the inning in the TV ballgame, then asked, "Well, what does my favorite grandson want now?"

He is my only grandson, so he just grinned. "Pops, you know I've got a birthday coming up pretty soon?"

"Now wait just one darned minute. I thought we talked this asking for presents business out three years ago. You agreed that you wouldn't do it any more. I thought you were growing up!"

He looked a little sheepish as he ducked his head. "Well, Mom said I could ask just this once."

"Oh," I said, "so your Mom is mixed up in this? How come she can't speak for herself?"

"She said you'd be more apt to do it if we asked."

"So, now it's we? I suppose Karin is mixed up in this too?"

With that my eight-year-old granddaughter ran in from the hallway. She threw herself in my lap and put both arms around my neck. "You will, won't you, Daddy Pops?"

"Okay, but remember I've been away for a long time on that trip; I don't have too much money to spend just now. Maybe I'll have to make whatever it is do for both your birthdays."

"Karin, you get out of here! Mom told me to do this. I'll do it myself." Eric was his usual self. No girl was going to interfere in his business.

"I am too going to stay. This is just as much for me as it is for you!"

I saw my daughter looking around the corner nodding her head, so I put my arm around the little blond-headed figure as a shield against the domineering male. "All right, you kids start a fight and you'll get nothing. Now tell me what this is all about."

Eric spoke up: "We want you to get a tape recorder!"

There was a question in his voice. It was obvious from his tone that there was something else to come.

"Well, I guess that can be arranged. But it will have to do for both of you."

I started to say more, but Karin interrupted. "We want something else too. But it wont cost you anything!"

"Well, at least that's a relief. What gives? I can't remember when you kids asked for something that didn't cost me."

Eric pushed his sister away. "You get out of here. I started this. I don't need a girl helping me!"

"Well, get to it. I can hardly wait." I slapped Karin on the rump and pushed her away. "The tape recorder I can handle. I suppose you have one all picked out and put away waiting for me to pay for?"

"Sure," he grinned. "Dad helped us. He said to get a good one as you are going to have to use it a lot."

"Oh," I said. "I thought you probably wanted it to record your music lessons. But what am I supposed to do with it? I know darned well you don't want me to sing for you!"

Karin giggled from the doorway. "You got to tell stories."

"Shut up, Karin!"

"Pops, you know all those stories you used to tell us about our grandmother and her family in the gold-mining country? We want you to tell us those again and put them on tape this time."

So that was it. I made a long face, but I knew that I was hooked. Who could resist a request like that? Anyway it might solve a problem.

Some years before I had made an attempt to write of the gold country and of the people who had worked in the mines. To help in my literary efforts I had enrolled in a creative writing course at the Extension Division of the University of California, at Berkeley. Leonard Bishop, the well-known novelist, who was conducting the course, made a most pertinent remark to the class. After reading one of my stories, he said, "Calhoon, you tell a hell of a good story, but you can't write worth a damn!"

I knew that Bishop had been correct, but I still worried that the stories, which only I knew, would be lost. Recording the stories as I retold them to my grandchildren would at least relieve my mind. The history of the children's ancestors would be preserved. Who knows? One of the kids might find the material interesting enough to do something with it. At the very least they would have the material for a thesis to meet the requirement for their master's degree in either history or English, if and when that day arrived.

"Who gave you that idea?" I asked.

"My science teacher. I showed him some of those gold quartz samples you gave me. When I told him how you got them, he said to be sure to write the information down. I knew that you would not do that, so Mom said to get you to tell the stories again and we would record them."

"At first we wanted Dad to hide a microphone, but he said that we couldn't do anything sneaky. And Mom said that you used to have your own radio program, so a microphone would not bother you."

"You will do it, won't you, Pops?"

What could I say? They had just made me an offer that I could not refuse!

AUTHOR'S NOTE: The literal transcript of the tapes has been altered in the interest of readability. The history of the Gold Rush family was recorded as conversation. As such, a great amount of extraneous material was included. At only a few points was dialogue allowed to remain in the text, and then only for dramatic effect. Mainly this is a straightforward account of the mining of gold in the hills of California, and of the people who dug for that elusive metal—the metal that so many have cursed as "the root of all evil."

Part 1

GOLD!

1

In the Beginning

Michael McGuire and Mary Cavanaugh were married in Ireland sometime late in 1847. They disembarked from a ship that docked in Philadelphia on January 24, 1848. By coincidence, this was the exact date on which the dour Scotsman James Marshall picked the yellow flakes from the cracks in the bedrock on the bottom of the millrace he was building on the American Fork in California. The Irishman and the Scotsman had never heard of each other, and they were destined never to meet, yet their lives were to be interwoven in a remarkable way. Marshall left no known descendants to perpetuate his line. His story died with him. McGuire, however, had read his Bible. He took seriously the admonition to "go forth and populate the earth." He did his best to obey!

The newlyweds had sailed from Belfast on or shortly before the tenth day of January. The ceremony had been solemnized in County Cork, and it would have taken several days for the horse drawn coach to reach Belfast by the circuitous route we surmise they followed to keep from being overtaken by the pursuing sheriff.

Michael was running from the law. Of that we are sure. Why he was running he refused to tell his children even after he had reached the age where he no longer needed to fear being returned to stand trial. He remained silent even after he knew that nothing he could have done would have diminished the respect his children held for him. Mary, in turn, refused to talk of his difficulties even after he had been in his grave for more than ten years.

Unlike the majority of the migrating Irish of the time, Mc-

3

Guire was not fleeing to escape starvation during the great potato famine. He seemed to have been rather affluent. Hunger had not forced him to leave his home. The cause may have been political, though it would seem not, as he would not have been reluctant to speak of that. He was a large man physically, so it is entirely possible that he had killed a man in a pub brawl, or in a fight over a girl. But since that offense could lead to extradition, murder was most probably not the cause. The second most likely crime would have been horse stealing. But that too was a hanging offense, and extraditable. We are left to wonder.

It is much more likely that he married against the wishes of the father of the bride. Many facts point to Mary's having been better educated and obviously from a higher social status than he was. Quite probably she had married the tall, dark, handsome son of old Ireland without society's approval. This was a crime in Ireland at that time, but not in the "Colonies." So once aboard ship and out of Irish waters, they were safe. Extradition was not possible.

Mary seemed to have very little in common with the women with whom she would have to associate in the New World. The difference in educational background led to a lack of understanding between Mary and her neighbors. Michael was hampered to some extent by her lack of sociability. The children of the union were most certainly affected. Even the grandchildren's lives were materially altered by the fact that Mary and Michael were never fully accepted into the social life of the community.

Funds were not lacking. When they arrived in America, the McGuires were able to purchase a farm on the outskirts of Philadelphia, and because they had arrived so early in the year, Michael could and did plant and harvest a crop during 1848.

Seemingly, the new immigrants were destined to become prosperous farmers in the new world. But Fate had other plans.

Early in December, 1848, Michael rode into Philadelphia on routine business. Hours before Mary had expected his return he dashed into the farm yard and, without stopping to care for his well lathered mount, rushed into the farmhouse kitchen.

Mary gasped when she saw the headlines in the paper he

handed her. "Here, read this," he said in a voice tense with excitement. "PRESIDENT VERIFIES DISCOVERY OF GOLD IN CALIFORNIA!"

Immediately her eyes moved to the subheadlines. "Kit Carson Arrives in Washington with Bag of Gold Nuggets! Philadelphia Mint Assays the Metal and Pronounces It GOLD of the Highest Purity!"

She bit her lip for the smallest part of a minute. Michael noticed her paling ever so slightly. Then, without a word, she turned and disappeared into the bedroom. In a moment she was back. "Here," she said. "Michael, I have not been a good wife to you. I did have a few cheap jewels when we married. I sold them and kept the money for an emergency. Get right back on that horse ride into town as fast as you can. Get two tickets on the first boat leaving for California. Every ship in port will be leaving fully loaded within the month. You must get there first to get us space!"

As Michael was to learn and relearn during his married life, there is no way to predict the reaction of a woman. Most especially not that of an Irish woman. He was taken completely by surprise. He had expected a stormy scene when he informed her that he must be off for the new goldfields. Instead, here she was insisting that they leave at once!

He could only stammer, "Mary, me love, you'll be the death of me yet. Sure, and I'll never understand you. Here I was riding all the way home rehearsing just what I must say and now you take the words right out of me mouth! But you can't go. I got the last ticket on the Panama-bound ship. The captain simply would not think of taking a woman. And you being seven months pregnant! I'd have to be a thousand kinds of a fool to take you into the tropics to cross to the Pacific. And God alone knows what the living conditions will be like in the goldfields."

Mary thought of a hundred reasons why she should not let her husband of less than a year out of her sight. But in spite of her romantic nature she forced herself to listen to the voice of reason. Even had she not been expecting so soon, she knew that she could only be a hindrance to her man in his dash to get to the gold country ahead of the ten thousand others who would start almost at once. If given the chance, of course, she could have kept the pace. Instinctively she knew that women would go with their men to California, often supplying the moral force needed to keep them pushing ahead after all hope of survival seemed lost. But with a baby to be born on the way? No. Michael was right. Send him. She could join him later if he succeeded in finding enough gold to make the journey worthwhile.

She handed him the money. "Here, take this. You'll have to pay for the passage. Get back to town before the shipping company sells your space to a higher bidder. I'll stay here and run the farm until you get back. The Sullivan boys will do the work for me. One of the girls will stay with me so I'll not be alone, and their mother will be here when the baby comes."

A smile seemed to flit across her face. It was a smile of anticipation and of sadness. "You take the money. Go on and get rich. I'll have a great big baby boy waiting for you when you get back!"

Michael pushed the money away. "The passage is all paid for as far as Panama, and I have the money to get from there on to California!"

"Oh, Michael. You can't have. We just did not have that much, and I know that there is not a banker in the world who would lend anyone passage money on the possibility of his finding gold."

Now it was his turn to surprise her.

"The minute I saw this paper I made a deal with Alvin Jones, the storekeeper we have been dealing with since we got here. I told him that I would guard a shipment of supplies to California and see that they were sold at a profit. He only had to pay for my passage. He jumped at the chance. After all expenses are paid, including my traveling expenses, we will divide the profits. Right now he is out buying up every pick and shovel in Philadelphia. Most probably there will be a lot of other things in short supply in California, but we do know that these will be needed desperately. Maybe the dumb Irish farmer you married will turn out to be not so too stupid after all!"

Mary's eyes flashed. "Michael McGuire, don't you ever let me hear you say such a thing again! You're not dumb, else why would I have married you? And as for being a farmer, if you're a good one, and I know that you are one of the best, it is something to be proud of, not something to be ashamed of! Don't you ever let me hear you saying the likes of that again, or I'll deliver a girl, not a boy!" With that, she began to cry and rushed into the bedroom.

He followed her and held her gently in his arms. "All right, me love." He kissed her and wiped away the tears. "Now don't you be fretting about it being a girl." He pressed his hand on her swollen stomach. For the first time he felt a strong kick. "No," he grinned, "It has to be a boy. No girl ever had a kick like that!"

The next week was filled with the hundred things that had to be done before he sailed. First, the Sullivans, their next neighbors to the west, had to be engaged to care for Mary and for the farm until he returned or until Mary could join him on the Pacific Coast. Crops had to be sold, and livestock reduced to a minimum. Finally, Mary's finances had to be settled. Jones, Michael's "partner" would be happy to oversee all her business dealings. Not that she was not capable, but a woman with a husband could not legally transact any business without her husband's signature. Jones must be given power of attorney to act in his place. Lastly, Michael must help in overseeing the loading of the merchandise.

Michael originated the idea of shipping only the pick heads and the shovel blades. He reasoned that wooden handles could be made at the mines. Why take up all that valuable shipping space with wood? This one idea was responsible for more than doubling the profits of the venture.

Several times before he sailed from the docks of Philadelphia on the morning of February 5, 1849, Michael was tempted to give up the whole wild scheme. How could he run off and leave the most beautiful girl in the world, especially now that she was about to give him a son? Had he not been so occupied in the preparations for the trip he might well have succumbed to the very real temptation to abandon the search for the elusive gold. The temptation became increasingly real as offers came from well-financed men wanting to take his place aboard ship. They were wildly eager to pay for the privilege. The initial offer of $500 did not tempt him too greatly, but when the bidding reached $2,000, he hesitated. In retrospect, he found that the average man heading for the goldfields would have been wise to have accepted the offer. Not one in a hundred of the "Argonauts" ever returned to the East with that much profit from several years of the most grueling labor under the most uncomfortable and dangerous conditions.

But Michael was not an average man. Mary knew this well. When he told her of the potential profit on his cabin space, she made the decision.

"No, Michael. You must go now. Sure, and the money would be nice. But if you missed your chance to get there ahead of the crowd, and later found that by being first you would have found a fortune in gold, I could never forgive myself for not sending you. I know that it is not the money that is holding you. You're a darling to think of me. But you must go!"

2

California!

McGuire reached Colón on the Gulf shore of the Isthmus ahead of the great rush. He quickly chartered a boat to take him and his mining tools to the head of navigation of the Charges River. The rest of the journey to the Pacific was made by mule train.

Fortunately the government had initiated the California Mail Service just months before the discovery of gold. He had only a ten-day wait before he found the planks of a steamer deck beneath his feet once more. He was on the last stage of his long journey—a journey that, if postponed only one month, would have required another half year to complete.

If the government had delayed the beginning of the steamer service up the Pacific Coast, thousands of men would have died of tropical disease, in the pesthole called Panama, while they waited to be picked off the beaches by chance ships in the California trade. As it was, well over fifteen percent of the gold-mad men succumbed to the ravages of malaria and of yellow fever while they waited for a chance to fight their way aboard every northbound ship that did touch that forlorn port.

When the fog cleared, and the ship made its way slowly through the passage called by Frémont "The Golden Gate," Michael was astonished by the forest of masts standing, stark and shorn of all sails, above the ships abandoned in the Bay. Their masters, their mates, and all their crews had deserted to rush headlong to the hills, where they had been told they could reap their fortune in golden nuggets with no more labor than stooping over to pick them out of the stream gravel. The crews, in particular, did not wait for the anchor to be dropped before they confiscated the small boats, swung them over the side, and rowed madly away toward the little town of Yerba Buena, now called San Francisco, to ask the way to the American Fork, where the gold was to be had.

When Michael arrived in April, 1849, the town of San Francisco was just beginning to be repopulated. Sam Brannon, the renegade Mormon, off the Pilgrim ship the *Brooklyn*, had started almost every one of the original inhabitants stampeding to the hills when it had suited his purpose to do so. He did this by simply verifying Dr. Semple's original announcement in his *California Star* that gold had been discovered on the American Fork!

Brannon, after weeks of denying, via the front pages of his competing newspaper, that there was any gold to be found, had reversed his position. Now he rode into town shouting "GOLD!" —proving his point by displaying a double handful of nuggets.

A mad rush to the hills along the American had resulted. But now the merchants, the saloonkeepers, the whores, and even the soldiers from the Presidio, who had deserted their posts to seek their fortunes, were returning. All had found that gold was indeed there, but that it took a great amount of back-breaking, dirty, dangerous work to get it. Sobering thoughts had brought them straggling back to the "city" that obviously would develop on the San Francisco Peninsula—a city touched by the hand of destiny to become one of the leading commercial and cultural centers of the world. They were back to help build that city.

McGuire tested the market for his mining tools in the town. He was astonished by the offers he received, but rumors of even higher prices upriver led him to transfer his shipment to a riverboat bound for Sutter's Fort on the American River two miles above its junction with the Sacramento.

The Riverboat did not go directly to the fort. Instead it tied up just below the mouth of the American. Here on the low-lying banks of the meandering principal stream of the valley were already the beginnings of a new city—a city later to be called Sacramento.

Fortune smiled on McGuire. The boat was met by a trader

from the north who was trying to buy supplies for his new store on the Yuba River near where it joined the Feather River. He knew that there might be supplies aboard that had not been consigned. He was there to make the agent or the owner an offer he could not refuse. Michael tested the market once more at the fort, but he found that he could get an additional twenty percent by staying aboard and accompanying his picks and shovels up river.

Too late he realized that if he had taken Mary's money and bought anything, preferably mining supplies, but anything that could have been shipped, he could have returned to Pennsylvania on the next boat a relatively rich man. Even the most frivolous of luxuries could have been sold at an enormous profit. In fact, the more frivolous the item and the more luxurious, the greater the profit would have been. Gold was literally being thrown away. A hundred dollars for a bottle of second-grade French wine was commonplace, and a thousand for a fancy dress for one of the saloon girls caused not the lifting of an eyebrow.

For a moment Michael was tempted to dispose of his supplies and rush back to purchase more and enter into the California trade. He realized, however, that by the time he could make the round trip others would be ahead of him. Any sizable shipment would have to come via the Horn. A full year must elapse before he could arrive back on the Pacific Coast. Surely, by that time the market would be well supplied.

With bags of gold being tossed about so carelessly, he decided that the risk was too great. Better to start looking for a mine of his own before they were all gone.

Almost hourly a fresh rumor spread of the fabulous nuggets to be picked out of the gravels of the Yuba, the Feather, or the Bear rivers, or from the smaller bars of the tributaries of each. All too often the rumors proved to be true. The bearded miners, flush with success, rushed to the first saloon in Sacramento or in the nearby mining camp, smashed their pokes open and spilled pounds of gold on the improvised bars, then demanded the best of everything for the "house"!

"By God, I can afford it. And when this is gone I know where there is a thousand times more!"

No wonder crude shovels sold for ten times their cost in the East. No wonder, in the actual diggings, the pick head or the metal blade of the shovel often traded at the rate of an ounce of gold for each pound of metal in the tool!

Michael had but a single problem. The offer for his tools was based on a ten percent down payment in gold dust at fifteen dollars per ounce. Then an additional payment of ten percent was due on the first of each succeeding month. A short visit to Sutter's Fort assured him that this was the common practice in California. The risks were great, but so too were the profits. He might never return from the mines. He must depend on the honesty of the buyer to forward the money to his wife if he failed to survive the dangers of the mountains. Or the buyer might die, or he might lose his money for any one of a hundred reasons in the highly fluctuating market, in which case he, McGuire, might lose. So he was told by the "Captain," and so he found to be the common practice in the new country.

That the buyer would simply refuse to pay was unthinkable. When that had happened at the very beginning of the rush, the defrauded man had told his story around camp. Then he had simply walked into the dishonest man's place of business and shot him!

A miner's court was assembled within the hour. If the evidence was good, the jury struck a quick bargain. The defendant could buy drinks all around, and go free; or he could spend two days in jail for "probable justified homicide."

With a system like that in operation, very few debts were ever welched on!

John Bidwell, a former Sutter employee, was at the fort. He quickly explained the system to McGuire, and assured him that, "barring some unforseen catastrophe," he would be paid in full. True, the country was already being overrun by thieves and cutthroats, but that kind did not go into the business of merchandising.

Commerce in the new land had to operate on a system of

mutual trust. Before gold had been discovered, the Mexican land-owners and the few American traders at Yerba Buena, at Monterey, and in and around San Pedro, acted as their own bankers, issuing notes that passed as legal tender. The system had grown, and the gold rush merchants could do no other than follow their example.

Captain Sutter had taken advantage of the system and had, within a period of only ten years, built up a fortune of untold millions. Now if he could only keep what was rightfully his, he must be rated one of the richest men in the world. The Captain almost never paid any of his debts, but why should he when a simple note, one secured by some portion of his vast holdings, passed from hand to hand as paper money?

Bidwell, himself had used the system to get started on his twenty-thousand-acre ranch on Chico Creek. When gold had been discovered on the American River, he had made a quick trip to Coloma to verify the discovery and to see how the gold was mined. Then he had taken a band of his Indians to the Feather River, where it flooded out of the mountains, just to the east of his ranch. There, with their labor, he had panned out $100,000 in coarse gold within two months. But he was not interested in mining. He used his gold to pay all of his debts. Now in 1849, he was busy getting ready to develop his good farm-land to produce the food that was in great demand. He knew that it would have to be supplied in even greater amounts when the mass of humanity came pouring down out of the Sierra moun-tain passes late that fall. He was one of the few to realize that near starvation would result when California was suddenly called upon to feed some fifty thousand new mouths.

Bidwell was sure that greater and more permanent fortunes were to be made from ranching than most men could ever hope to make, and to keep, by digging for gold.

"Invest your money in good land," he told McGuire. "In ten years you'll be a very rich man. Mining is a risky business. Farm-ing on our rich river bottom land cannot fail. The richest land in the world can be had for twenty-five cents an acre. One good crop and your land and all your improvements are paid for! From

then on you have the surest "mine" in the world. You can bring
your family out and live like the landed gentry of Ireland, except
that your realm will stretch for miles. Compared to your holdings, the largest estate in Ireland will look like the stall of a child's
pony."

Bidwell followed his own advice. He soon was living in semi-
feudal splendor. Eventually he became a United States senator.
He was a presidential candidate in 1886.

McGuire listened, but he did not hear. Instead the siren's
song of wealth in the streambeds blotted all other sounds from
his ears. He had been bitten by the "gold bug"! With the "luck
of the Irish" on his side, he could not fail. Unlike the spend-
thrift miners, who threw their gold to the winds, he would keep
what he found.

So Michael McGuire must become a miner. His background
and his previous experiences had equipped him no better for the
task at hand than were the two thousand men who had preceded
him into the hills. Nor were the hundred thousand who were to
follow him during the next two years any better informed. He,
as did most of the others, trusted to blind luck in his search for
riches.

There were exceptions to this lack of knowledge of how to
go about the task at hand. One or two of the early arrivals had
mined placer gold in the mountains of the Carolinas. There
the poor white farmers, competing against slave labor, found that
they could add a few dollars to their annual income by washing
the gravel of their mountain valley streams. They worked in the
winter when there was little farm work to do. The recovery of an
ounce of gold after a full month of digging was considered excellent. Now, their earlier experiences were well repaid. They
knew how to go about getting the fine gold "dust," which could
not be picked up with the fingers or on the point of a hunting
knife.

One of these "hillbillies," George Humphries, jumped ship in
mid-1848. He bought a pick and a shovel at Sutter's Fort before
taking to the hills, but his attempt to buy a gold pan was met
with a blank stare from the storekeeper. Such a thing had never

been heard of in California. Humphries shrugged his shoulders and made do with the largest frying pan that was to be had. This worked after a fashion. It was not efficient, but he was able to demonstrate that plenty of gold was being missed by the unskilled miners.

He returned to the fort. There he was able to get a blacksmith to forge him a pan, one with the sloping sides so familiar in every picture of the forty-niners. Back at the diggings, the ease with which he recovered the gold and the amount of fine gold added to his poke made him the envy of every man who fancied himself a miner.

McGuire accepted the offer of Isaiah Collins, the trader from upriver, and stayed aboard the little riverboat as it worked its way to the confluence of the Sacramento and Feather rivers, then another twenty miles up that much smaller stream, to the mouth of the Yuba. Navigation was possible for only half a mile on that stream, so at that point the boat made fast to the northern bank, and the city of Marysville was founded.

Once ashore, Michael lost no time going about the business of learning the rudiments of gold mining. He walked along the banks of the Yuba River to the point where it emerged from the hills onto the broad plains of the Sacramento Valley. He found every bar already being mined by the early arrivals. He also found that some of the smaller streams that emptied into the main channel were even richer than the river itself. Rumor told him that the Yuba and its three branches had already been prospected far back into the mountains. It seemed best to try for a tributary that had not as yet been prospected.

Within a day he had seen enough. He had learned all that he could from the men working the river sand and gravel. He had watched them diverting the water from the river to wash the gravel from the adjoining bars, exposing the bedrock, then turning the water back into the main channel. Now it had become a simple matter to pick up the gold.

Two of the miners out of the hundred he saw working the river gravel had pans. They were recovering several times as much gold with little or no more work as were those without the tools to recover the fine gold, or even those who were trying to imitate their method with frying pans.

Michael returned to the boat landing where Collins had already set up a store in a tent. Again his luck held. Collins had no pans, nor did he have the material from which they could be made, but the riverboat had not as yet cast off for the downstream run. In the engine room he found a piece of flat iron. It cost him but a bottle of whiskey. (It is remarkable that alcohol was always to be had. No matter how short food, clothing, and the supplies necessary for mining might be, strong drink was always available. The explanation was that good whiskey was rated a necessity. It was about the only medicine available—medicine for both the physical and the spiritual needs of the isolated men in the wilderness.)

The iron was not for sale at any price, so only the "Sweet talk" of one who had kissed the Blarney Stone, made more potent by the sound of good Irish whiskey gurgling from the mouth of a bottle into a glass held close to the nose of the engineer, caused the precious metal plate to disappear before the boat cast off for San Francisco Bay.

Michael found an anvil and a hammer and beat out a crude pan. Fortunately the sheet iron was made of malleable material. Had it been cast iron, as were most iron products of the time, it would have been brittle. A forge would have been required. He did heat the metal as much as possible, but, lacking charcoal, he was forced to use the coals of a manzinita fire. This was a trick the "Mountain Men" brought to the California scene. They had mended their traps and shod their horses using the hot embers of mountain greasewood to soften the iron. Later, in California and in Oregon, they found that that the dried stems of the red-barked brush made an even hotter fire.

On April 24, 1849, McGuire packed his mining tools and his bedroll on the back of a horse one of the Hawaiian boys had caught and had broken to the saddle and to the pack.

Long before Marshall had made his discovery, numerous natives of the Sandwich Islands were working the ports and sailing the ships along the California coast. They too rushed to the mines. However, they found that mining was completely foreign to their mode of making a living. They were oriented to the sea and to a more adventurous life. They turned to manning the riverboats, and to living off the unbelievable "runs" of fish in the rivers. Already they had established a fishing village on the west bank of the Feather River just below its junction with the Yuba. Fishing was their main occupation, but they soon found that it was profitable to trap the wild Spanish horses at isolated waterholes. In addition they found that riding the pitching and plunging of the maddened beasts as they tried to dislodge their tormentors from their backs, provided the risk and the adventure they missed, now that they could no longer stake their lives against the curling crashing waves of the north shores of Oahu!

Michael, with a horse to carry his supplies, was the envy of almost every other miner in the hills. Mostly they had to pack their food, their bedrolls, and their mining tools on their own backs. Not that many of them could not afford horses. They were just not available at any price. Wild horses were everywhere abundant, but they were hard to catch and still harder to tame.

At the mouth of a creek flowing into the river from the south just below Tim Buctoo's diggings, he stopped at a spot where the earlier miners had washed away the gravel and had picked up all the visible gold. With his freshly sharpened pick he dug out the fine material from each of the cracks in the bedrock. Carefully, he swept the broken bits of rock into his pan. Then he squatted by a small pool of clear water to make the first attempt at panning gold. He took his time and worked the pan with great care. He saved some gold but when he repanned the tailings he found that he had missed some. It had washed over the side of the pan along with the heavier bits of rock. By repeated attempts he found his errors and within hours gained the confidence needed to manipulate the pan so that only the waste material was washed away. The gold remained in the pan.

He had not the slightest idea of how to weigh the gold he did recover, but going by the miner's rule—"a pinch equals a dollar"— he estimated that he could make at least a dollar an hour by this method of simply cleaning up after the earlier miners who had scorned the fine gold in their rush to get on to another bar where the nuggets were reported to be the size of pigeon eggs.

Michael was forced to agree with them. Just three short months before he would have thought himself on the verge of a fortune had he been able to earn ten dollars per day. Now that he knew where and how he could make enough to live on, he had to gamble for much higher stakes. In any case the mined-over spots would soon be gone. Shortly all miners would have gold pans. They were bound to scrape the bedrock once they had it exposed. No one could make a living gleaning the fine gold from the bedrock after they had finished. (Later the Chinese did just that. But they worked harder and longer, and for only a dollar or two a day.)

No one in California had the slightest idea as to the source of the gold found in the stream gravel. Consequently, no one had the faintest notion as to where to look for the best places with the richest deposits. Prospecting was a hit-and-miss-proposition. The searcher either looked for a place on a stream that was already being mined and that had as yet escaped the shovel and the pan, or he found a stream that had not been mined and started digging.

At first, the testing of a stream consisted of throwing some gravel into a pan and washing it in a nearby pool. If considerable gold was left in the crease between the flat bottom of the pan and the sloping sides, a claim was staked and the work of removing the waste dirt to get at the gravel beneath was commenced.

Most streams had some gold. But it was often overlooked because the major amount of the gold present lay on the surface of the bedrock, usually under a deep layer of dirt and barren gravel. So luck played a great part in prospecting. One man might pan a creek with no results. Another following a day behind, might pan gravel from only a few feet from the first sample, and pick a stray nugget from his pan, and the "rush" would be on!

McGuire was surprised by the number of men working the river bars. How so many had reached California ahead of him he could not imagine. The deserted ships in the bay were only a partial explanation. He did not know that several hundred families bound for Oregon in the summer of 1848 had changed their route when they had been met by Kit Carson at Fort Hall on the Snake River. Carson had been on his way to Washington with a bag of nuggets to confirm that gold had indeed been found in paying quantities in the territory so recently taken from Mexico. Later hundreds more familes left their Willamette Valley farms in Oregon to thread their way through the passes of the Siskiyou Mountains, past Mount Shasta, and down the canyon of the Sacramento River and on into the gold country.

Already several ships had made the long voyage across the Pacific, and had returned loaded with Orientals from the coastal cities of China. More ships had made several round trips to the Sandwich Islands (Hawaiian), returning each time loaded with islanders, and with sailors off the whalers who had put into the islands for supplies, only to lose their crews just as had the ships in San Francisco Bay when the news of GOLD was circulated.

But by far the majority of the new arrivals came from Mexico and from the west coast countries of South America. The Mexicans arrived first. Mostly they came from the state of Sonora. There they had mined some gold and knew the rudiments of the trade. They were highly successful along the rivers of the "southern mines." When ships loaded with the South American miners arrived, their passengers and their crews naturally rushed to the area where Spanish was the dominant language. Shortly, all Spanish-speaking miners were called "Chilanos." The Yankees could see no difference in their racial characteristics, nor in their social backgrounds. None of these hard-working "foreigners" had as yet migrated north of the American. Michael had no competition from them.

Michael continued upriver until he came to the mouth of Deer Creek. This stream he followed to Caldwell's Store, where rich gravel had been reported. He walked over a hundred places where skilled miners recovered from ten to a hundred ounces per day, once they had learned to use the more sophisticated tools of mining. He found only a few bars, however, where "ground sluicing" and panning would be practical. He sampled the gravel, but did not dig deep enough to get at the heavy gold, so he continued on upstream.

In only rare places was the surface gravel worth working with a pan alone. Years later, he laughed with the others at the story of the veterans of Colonel Stevenson's New York Regiment, who prospected Auburn Ravine and found only a few colors. Later, at Thompson's Dry Diggings in the Ravine, the six inches of gravel that lay immediately above the bedrock often produced $100 per pan. Had the ex-soldiers known the rudiments of prospecting, every man who had been discharged from the regiment in California because it had arrived too late to fight the Mexicans in the 1846 War would have gone home with a thousand times his army pay in his pockets.

At Caldwell's Store (later Nevada, and, finally, Nevada City) the creek swarmed with miners. Each was recovering from one to ten ounces per day. There was no room for new men in the narrow channel. The rich Eocene gravel lying under the overburden of volcanic ash on the higher banks of the creek had not as yet been discovered. Had Michael arrived only a few months later, he might have joined the thousand men who were "coyoting" on the rich plateau. There, the bedrock was so studded with gold that claims were limited to ten feet by ten feet. Even so, from the hundred square feet, $10,000 to $25,000 in coarse gold was often recovered. The mining was done by digging straight down as with a water well. At bedrock, the gravel was picked away from under the surrounding area, leaving unsupported ground above. Cave-ins often occurred. The poor crushed miner was always dug out and given a decent burial. The bedrock was too rich to be used as a tomb!

Michael was not easily discouraged, but he was quick to see that working known creeks was not apt to gain him wealth in a hurry. He would try new country while there was yet time. Then if his luck did not hold, he would take Bidwell's advice and return to farming. There he was skilled. He knew that the California pioneer had been right. He could not fail.

On May 5th, he worked his way straight south over the low ridge at Town Talk. Then he made his way down into the valley of Wolf Creek. At once he found gold, but again the easily worked bars had been staked. At the mouth of Rhode Island Ravine, Lamarque, a French Canadian who had mined in Mexico, had already set up a trading post complete with a bar where, wonder of wonders, he was serving Irish whiskey!

Michael had once spent a little time in France. His French was pathetic, and Lamarque spoke only a dialect that would have passed for a foreign language on the streets of Paris, but in this far place the two "foreigners" had to become friends. With the very limited English of the Hudson Bay Company Trappers, Lamarque had tried to explain to the early arrivals how mining on the small creeks should be done. The arrogant ex-sailors who had flocked to this area were not about to be told anything. How could it be possible for a man who could not even speak English to tell them anything?

Within a day, using Michael's French, and a great deal of sign language, Lamarque had demonstrated how to keep from overlooking the gold in the small streams, which he knew the miners were missing. Then he sent McGuire a half mile downstream and up a small brook known as Little Wolf Creek. This joined the main stream from the east.

McGuire found gold at every prospect hole as he worked his way up the canyon of the little stream. The amount of gravel in the spots he sampled was too small to be of interest. He had to find a relatively level area where a large amount of gravel had accumulated. On the evening of the second day he broke out into a small mountain meadow just at the base of Osborn Hill. He picketed his horse in the lush grass along the stream and prepared to make camp for the night. In doing so he dug out two rather large stones to be used as supports for his cooking pots. He noticed some gravel immediately under the stones. On a hunch he shoveled some of the material into his gold pan and washed it in the gurgling stream.

"Good God be praised!" he shouted before he had washed

more than two-thirds of the waste gravel over the side of the pan. His fingers had come into contact with "stones" that were much too heavy to be anything but GOLD!

A hundred dollars per pan was what every prospector dreamed of. He had hit it and more! All thought of supper was forgotten. He dug and panned until darkness made it impossible for him to see the gold that accumulated in the crease of the pan. Only then did he pause to take stock of his surroundings. True, no more large nuggets showed up to "growl" in the pan. (Large nuggets tend to drag across the bottom of the pan. In doing so, they produce much deeper vibrations than do the lighter quartz pebbles.) Even so, several pans gave up more than ten dollars. His fortune was made. Through the deepening twilight, he could see that the "flat" contained twenty to thirty acres. Even so, if only a small portion of it carried gold in paying quantities, the total would be staggering. (Actually only about five acres carried enough gold to make mining pay.)

Michael slept but little that night. The slightest scurrying of a pack rat in the brush brought him to full wakefulness. He interpreted every sound to be that of someone who was about to make a claim on his find before he could stake it and file his claim with the local mining committee.

At the first showing of light on the eastern horizon, he was up. The adrenalin was flowing too fast to allow him to cook and eat more than a few bites for breakfast. Even those he had to force himself to swallow. He realized that he had to work fast. Later in the day he would have time for eating.

Where the meadow gave way to the canyon cut by the little creek, he drove a stake and built a three-foot pile of rocks around it. To the stake he attached a paper protected by an oil cloth. The paper stated that he, Michael McGuire, had discovered gold at this location on May 7, 1849, at 6:00 post meridian. He did, therefore, claim the next hundred feet along the creek bed running in an easterly direction. The claim was to extend to the top of the slopes to the north and to the south. He promised faithfully to perform the work on the claim as prescribed by the local mining committee. Notice was thereby given that anyone trespassing on the claim must suffer whatever penalty the local *alcalde* (justice of the peace) might assess. Next he dug discovery holes at ten foot intervals along the creek channel. He did not stop to pan the dirt. That would come later.

At a hundred feet above the first discovery stake he drove another, and built a similar rock marker. On this stake he posted two notices: one for the original claim, and a similar notice bearing Mary's name. Still another hundred feet upstream, he repeated the process. This time he put the claim in the name of Joseph McGuire. As he did so he uttered a short prayer: "Dear Jesus. Please let there be a son back in Pennsylvania. Amen."

The claim in Mary's name was most probably quite illegal by the rules in force at that time, and the one in Joseph's name had not the slightest chance of being ruled legal even had he been sure that he had a son. But under the circumstances he did not want any close neighbors. He was sure that he could build up a reputation for being a wild-eyed Irishman should anyone question the ownership of any of the claims. Presently, at least, good claims were too easy to come by for anyone to resort to claim jumping when the irate owner was close at hand.

One more step had to be taken before the claims were legally his. He rode his horse as fast as possible down the steep hillside to the valley of Wolf Creek. There, in Lamarque's store, he posted a very rough description of the claims. The storekeeper protested vigorously. "Only one," he said in French. Michael suddenly lost all of his knowledge of that language.

He took Lamarque aside and showed him the size of one of the nuggets found in his first pan. He bought, and presented the Canadian with, a bottle of the best whiskey in the store. When the contents of the bottle had mellowed their friendship, he discovered that he could speak French once more. He assured Lamarque that his wife and son would shortly be in San Francisco waiting for him to build shelter so that they could join him at the claim. He conveniently forgot to say that his wife, even if she were there, would most certainly not be seen working in the mud and the water of a mining claim. He also forgot to explain that he was not sure that he had a son, and in any case the boy was only a few months old. It would be some time before he could shovel gravel and twist a pan.

He also explained that before California had become United States territory, with the assurance that local customs and laws would be honored, it had been possible for women to own property in their own name. That had been the law under Mexican rule. That was what he would expect Lamarque to tell anyone who might object to a claim being registered in a woman's name. Then he asked Lamarque to ride back with him and stake and file a claim above him on the creek.

Lamarque thanked him but refused. He had seen too many claims that had looked to contain a million become worthless after the first rich pocket had been mined out. He had gambled often enough. Now he had a sure thing. Let the wild-eyed, gold-crazed newcomers work in the mud. Let the greenhorns come down with the fevers and with the rheumatism. He had found an easier way to get the gold. His usual markup was one thousand percent. If that did not lead to riches fast enough, watered whiskey and a bevy of Mexican girls were infallible methods of making store keeping a very profitable business. Then, to be on the safe side, he had the only gold scales in the area. A set of weights, made ten percent heavier than their markings indicated, guaranteed a profit if all else failed.

With his claims now relatively safe, Michael celebrated. He joined Lamarque in seeing how fast they could empty the bottle, and drank to the health of several miners who wandered in. Fortunately, on the journey back to the claim, his horse remembered the good grass at "McGuire Flat." Michael managed to stay in the saddle by holding on with both hands. Certainly he could not have used just one hand to guide the horse, even if his eyes had been able to focus on the beginnings of a trail up Little Wolf Creek to the claims.

Once the headache had worn off the following morning, he began to prospect his claims in earnest. Again his fortune held. For a reason he did not understand until years later, the pay dirt vanished just above the upper edge of the last claim. This was in his favor. Now he need not worry about neighbors working downstream and jumping his ground.

At once he needed shelter. He had been told that he could expect little or no rain after the middle of May. He did not believe it. He could not conceive of a rainless climate. Because he was forced to work alone, it was impossible for him to build a cabin. His claims and the surrounding hillsides contained a wealth of timber, but the size of the trees made them unusable. The smallest was nearly three feet in diameter, much too large to be felled with the small axe he carried. Even if he had had the tools for felling such monsters, their sheer bulk made it impossible for him to move the logs into place. He was forced to build a lean-to, made up of a few hardwood saplings that grew beside the creek.

Michael had been given the correct information about the lack of rainfall during the California summer. Except for one slight drizzle there was no more rain at his claim after he arrived. By the middle of July, the drought had become real. The springs that fed his little stream dried up and only a trickle of water continued to flow. Without water, mining was impossible. Despite this he would make his permanent home in this new country. He fell in love at once with the green of the forests accented by the scent of the pines and the cedars. He knew that the dry heat of the long summers was the best remedy for the rheumatism that must follow working in the cold wetness of the placer mines.

Mary would love the life they could make for themselves here. What a fabulous place to live and to raise their family! He must bring her to California as soon as possible.

He had prospected the flat extensively enough to know that it would produce in excess of a tenth of an ounce of gold from each cubic yard of dirt washed. Although his mathematical education had been limited, it took no genius to calculate that he could expect about $1.50 from each square yard of bedrock on his claims. A quick measurement of the area showed that there was in excess of forty thousand square yards to be washed to bedrock. That, by any method of figuring, amounted to $60,000.

Then it dawned on him that his wealth was in the safest bank in the world. No one could steal it so long as he kept title to the land. The rise and fall of the world's business would never affect him. And best of all, he could not spend it foolishly. All he had to do was to work at mining a few months each year when water was available; then he and his family could do as they pleased for the remainder of the time. What a life he saw stretched out ahead!

All he now needed was for his family to be here, "and his cup would run over". He was resourceful enough to solve that problem.

His friendship with the French-speaking storekeeper now paid off in a big way. Lamarque promised to see that the claims were not jumped. He had just the man. Joe Jones, an ex-sailor who never could seem to find gold enough to quench his thirst, would do enough work under his supervision to keep the claim jumpers away. In return he was to have the little gold he panned out. McGuire was to guarantee the bar bill he would run up. Lamarque knew that the profit on that alone would more than pay him for his supervision. He also knew that if he allowed the claims to be jumped, McGuire would never pay the bar bill. It was a good bargain for both parties.

3

Problems of the Travelers

In August, McGuire rode down through the shimmering heat, and through the ankle-deep dust of the Sacramento Valley. Gone were the blue of the lupines and the gold of the California poppies from the endless fields. Gone was the belly-high grass of the lower foothills where his horse had to be forced to leave the shade of the last oaks of the valley rim. Only the green of the cottonwoods and willows, bordering the streams fed by the melting snows of the highest mountains to the east, broke the drabness and the glare of the straw-brown land.

The snow-clad peaks of the Sierras no longer beckoned the traveler to "come, rest in the coolness of their shade." Not since the middle of May, when the summer haze closed down over the interior valleys, had they been seen. Now the traveler found himself walking across a heat-deadened land enclosed by the gray walls of an inverted bowl—walls composed of dust-ladened air, which, like the end of the rainbow, seemed to move ever outward as the sojourner moved forward, bent on breaking through the barrier into a land that but such a short time before seemed surely to be the Garden of Eden.

Michael was forced to spend almost a full week in this torment before a river steamer pushed off from the riverbank, bound for Sacramento and on to the cool fog of San Francisco Bay. Not until the first stirring of the sea breeze brushed against their faces as they entered Susuin Bay were the sweltering passengers to gain any relief from the summer torture. Ashore, they might gain some solace by finding a high dry place where some slight breeze usually developed before midnight, and where the mosquitoes

27

did not make life unbearable. Aboard the boat, however, there was no such relief. Only the toughest skin could repel the onslaught of the millions of biting, sucking insects. Those who were not equipped with this natural protection had to stay in their cabins. They had a choice: They could go on deck and be eaten raw, or they could stay indoors and slowly cook. Traveling in the California valleys during the heat of the summer was not a desirable adventure.

The town at the junction of the Yuba and the Feather rivers was now officialy known as Marysville. In April, there had been twenty-five people living there waiting to obtain an outfit for prospecting in the hills; or taking up permanent residence to serve the men going to and coming from the mines. Now in mid-August there were two hundred and fifty, and the prospects were that when the wagon trains from the Missouri arrived three months later the population would multiply several times.

Already a few fast riders, guided by old beaver trappers, had ridden down from the crest of the Sierras with tales of almost continuous wagon trains following the old Oregon Trail to Fort Hall on the Snake River, or taking the Hasting Cutoff through Salt Lake City. Farsighted men saw that the great influx of immigrants would have to be cared for until they could become self-sufficient. They meant to be on hand at strategic points to take advantage of the plight of the new arrivals.

The first of the overland rush arrived at Johnson's Ranch late in September, 1849. The ranch, located on the Bear River just where it spilled out of the bare brown foothills into the flood plains of the Sacramento, was the goal of the argonauts. When they left the Missouri on their great adventure, Sutter's Fort had beckoned them. But as the miles had stretched out endlessly, as their supplies had dwindled, and as their wagons had disintegrated in the dry sands of the deserts, and their draft animals had died of bad water, little or no food, and from simple overwork, the first bit of civilization in the wilderness became their point of focus.

The little city of Wheatland now occupies the greater part

of the original Mexican land grant made to the beaver trapper Bill Johnson. From this point the newly arrived miners made their way north or south to the rivers where they might find the "Golden Fleece." Frequently, a toss of a coin determined in which direction they should begin their search.*

Late in 1849, some enterprising promoters from Marysville laid out a better route from Emigrant Gap to the Sacramento Valley. Better for Marysville, that is! Instead of following the Valley of the Bear down the floor of the glaciated valley—a route that forced the wagons to cross the terminal moraines of the glacier—the Marysville guides took the wagons up the north bank of the Bear River Canyon to Washington Ridge. Once on the crest, they found a gentle grade all the way to Nevada City. The only obstacles were the four- to six-foot sugar pines and cedars that blocked their paths.*

From Nevada City, the road climbed the small ridge back of Grass Valley. It dropped down Squirrel Creek through Rough

---

*It was from Johnson's Ranch that the organized search parties had set out in their almost foolhardy attempts to rescue the Donner Party during the terrible winter of 1846. Knowing of no better routes, the forty-niners had followed the tracks of Donner's wagons up the Truckee River out of Nevada to Truckee Lake (Donner Lake). Then keeping to the south of the present Highway 80 and the Southern Pacific tracks, they crossed the crest of the mountains and worked their way down to Soda Springs on the upper reaches of the South Yuba River. Instead of following this stream, however, they crossed to the ridge south of the upper Bear River and followed the easy grade to Emigrant Gap. Here they lowered their wagons down the sheer rock face of the glacier-cut cliff to the smooth valley floor below. Steep Hollow Creek and the Greenhorn still presented broken country to cross, but mostly it was an easy downhill pull from there on. The Donner rescue parties had used this exact route in 1846. Not until after 1850 were lower and less rugged routes over the mountains known.

*State Highway 20 now follows the exact route. Remnants of the wagon train road are still clearly visible. Its circuitous route beside the arrow-straight modern highway testifies to the willingness of the pioneers to compromise with, rather than fight against, nature. The road circled the giants of the forest, and when it encountered a fallen monster, the pathfinders made no attempt to cut through. They bowed to a superior force and went around.

and Ready, through Penn Valley and followed Indian Valley to what a hundred years later became Camp Beale, then on to the south bank of the Yuba at Marysville.

From one of the first wagon trains to reach Marysville, Michael's merchant friend, Collins, purchased a team and wagon for his use on his return to California. Collins had his choice. Almost every member of the train arrived hungry and penniless. This was particularly true of the immigrants who had taken the route through Salt Lake City and on west, following the Hasting Cutoff straight across the Salt flats to the Humboldt River.*

McGuire's team and wagon came at a bargain price. The owner was desperate for food for his family. But when he found that he could have the use of the outfit until late in the following spring, he considered himself most fortunate.

Michael had commissioned Collins to buy household goods from the wagons for his use on his return. This proved to be far more difficult than finding the team and wagon. The women who had fought their way across the continent were made of sterner stuff. They had defied their husbands and the orders of the wagon train masters to throw away the useless things to lighten the loads. They simply refused to throw away their four-poster beds, their commodes, their rocking chairs, and their solid maple tables. Now that they had won, they were not about to give them up for a little food.

They could, and they would, wait one more day while their

---

*The Mormons had reoutfitted them for the hard, dangerous trip across the deserts and over the mountains ahead. They had advised the travelers well, and they had outfitted them to the best of their ability. Had they not done so, thousands would have died in the waterless wastes. The Mormons, however, needed money to build their new nation in the wilderness. The immigrants were going to the land of gold. They would need no money. They most certainly could not spend it on the way, so why let them carry it beyond the City of God? Prices were flexible. The immigrant had no choice. He could neither go ahead, nor could he go back without supplies. It was not a question of the asking price of food, or of the wagon wheels. Rather, the question was "How much did the buyer have?" Charity caused the good church people to give a poor family a desperately needed wagon for $10, while the next man in line had to pay $200 for one not so good!

menfolk went to work. Supplies were short in California, but labor was in even greater demand. An ounce of gold per day was the usual wage. If a man had any special skill, such as carpentry or blacksmithing, double that amount might be offered. The men could wait to get to the mines. They could go to work for a few weeks to get food for their wives and their children. No one was going to sell Aunt Anna's highboy for just a little food when a man could make as much in a day as he had ever made in a whole month before! Mrs. McGuire would have to make do when she arirved. She should have brought what she needed with her!

It is said that God looks after drunks, fools, and little children. His hand stayed the Pacific winter storms of 1849. Even the slowest parties and the most slovenly organized wagon train reached the summit of the Sierras and got through the passes made famous by Donner, Carson, and Bidwell, before the winter storms set in. Had the season been "normal," the thousands who would have perished at the base of the eastern escarpment of the "snowy, saw-toothed mountains" (the name given by the Spanish to the range that formed the eastern boundary of California) would have dwarfed the suffering of the Donner Party. Cannibalism might not have been limited to the few questionable cases in that ill-fated party of pioneers.

At Sacramento, the boat stopped to take on passengers and gold. The town had doubled in size since April. A "Californian" aboard muttered strong Spanish oaths as he pointed out the location of many of the buildings on the mud flats. "By January," he said, "the buildings that have not been washed away will be under twenty feet of water!"

The gold-mad traders would not listen when experienced men told them of the habits of the river. Each must place his store or saloon closest to the boat landings to be the first to tempt the newly arriving miners to spend their gold in his establishment.

The river was now at its lowest stage. Above Sacramento, great skill had been required to keep the boat in the deepest part of the channel. Even then it repeatedly grounded on mud flats and on sand bars, wasting precious time backing off and probing for deeper water. Below the mouth of the American, the volume of the water increased. This, added to the effects of the tides, which reached this far upriver on certain days, made for easier sailing on through the delta and out onto the salt water of the bay. Only six hours were required to thread the passageways through the peat islands and to gain the open water of Susuin Bay.

A hearty cheer went up. Away from the shores and marshes, the devilment of the mosquitoes was quieted, and each added mile brought more of the sea breeze, with the resulting dramatic drop in the temperature. The passengers found that early evening sleep was now possible, and each burrowed deeper under his blanket as the little boat rounded San Pablo Point and was buffeted by the cold dank winds off the Alaskan Current, sucked through the Golden Gate by the rising of the heated air of the interior valleys beyond.

The number of ships abandoned in the bay had quadrupled since Michael had arrived there only five months before. Once the shores of California were reached, almost no ship ever sailed again. The only exceptions being the government mail boats to and from Panama. The captains of these could, and often did, requisition sailors from the navy and soldiers from the Presidio to make up a crew. A few ships risked sailing westward to the Hawaiian Islands with skeleton crews, knowing that once there, whalers off stranded ships would gladly sign on for the prolonged voyage to the coast of China and back to California, a trip of some twenty thousand miles to cross the three thousand miles to the goldfields.

When it became known in Marysville that McGuire was returning to the East Coast, he was besieged by miners wanting him to deliver gold to their families, or at least mail letters there for quick delivery. He refused all requests save for the mailing of one letter for each. The gold was too heavy and too dangerous to transport. He was traveling light. A large amount of gold would have required an armed bodyguard. The gold he must take to pay his debt to the merchant who had advanced the money for his trip, and to pay all his necessary traveling expenses, he sewed between the lining and the upper leather of his boots. From that time on, he slept with his boots on.

In his money belt he carried only the amount needed for immediate expenses and to placate any holdup man who might accost him. Better let him think that his efforts had been worthwhile than have him suspect that he was carrying hidden money, in which case the bandit might well strip him of all his clothes, and probably kill him in the process.

In the mines, bags of gold dust could safely be left on the table in the miner's cabin while he was at work. Any stranger was welcome to come in, cook and eat a meal, and if he were without funds he was expected to take a pinch or two of the dust. To take more was unthinkable. Such morality did not hold true in the towns, and it most certainly did not exist in Sacramento or in San Francisco. Probably the most dangerous places of all were on the boats that touched at those ports.

Outbound passage from San Francisco presented no problem. Michael sailed for Panama aboard the mail boat within a week. At the Isthmus, he found all the traffic moving west, so he had no trouble crossing to Colón, nor was there any delay booking passage to New York. Homeward-bound ships were leaving almost daily.

His main fear was of being robbed. He did not talk of his successful mining, as did most of those who had found gold in rather large amounts. Rather, he indicated that he was on his way east to arrange credit and purchase supplies for the store he was supposed to have in Marysville.

Even with this precaution, he continued to sleep with his boots on, and with a loaded and primed pistol close at hand. It was no secret that the crews of the ships in the coastal trade had found it more profitable to "mine the miners," than to sweat for the gold in the cold waters of the Sierran streams. If all other means failed, they did not hesitate to commit robbery to get "their share" of the gold the passengers carried. If the passenger was known to be carrying enough, killing was not beyond their capabilities. Bodies were too easy to dispose of overboard to make the risk too great. Notices were posted on all ships that robberies were common, and that the passengers traveled at their own risks. Later, the ships carried safes, well guarded in the captain's quarters. Safe delivery of gold was guaranteed at the port of debarkation. Even then no really safe way was ever devised for getting gold across from Panama to Colón, save by hiring heavily armed guards.

Michael's ploy succeeded. Probably no weightier pair of boots, worn by a man with a lighter heart, had ever clomped down the gangplank onto the docks of New York.

4

The Reunion

Mary McGuire was in one of the deep funks so common to the temperamental Irish. Joe, the baby, was almost a year old. She was having a difficult time weaning him. To stop his whining the evening before, she had allowed him to nurse. Her breasts were almost dry. In his frustration, the infant had used his new teeth to vent his anger. In fact he had bitten her savagely!

To add to her physical woes, that morning she had found one of her best milk cows and an unborn calf dead following an unsuccessful attempt to make a breach delivery. She had warned Pat Sullivan, her helper, that conditions did not look good, and that he should keep a sharp eye on that particular animal. He had scoffed at the idea. "After all, what did a woman know about calving? Damned if he wasn't getting tired of being bossed around by a female. It was more than a man could bear!"

But Mary knew that her real trouble was the lack of any word from Michael. One letter had arived via Panama stating that he had arrived safely in San Francisco Bay. A month later a note had reached her saying that he was off to the mines. After that— nothing!

Every night she imagined him set upon by a band of painted, screaming Indians, of being devoured by a huge grizzly bear, or running for his life, pursued by a pack of savage wolves. Later she would laugh with him at her fears. The Digger Indians, whom she came to know, were most certainly no menace, and the grizzlies and the wolves of California did not inhabit the mining country. The only possible danger was from a black bear or from a mountain lion. But neither of these species would ever attack a man if not provoked. Still, she believed the stories—stories that prevail to this day. Her vivid imagination caused her many sleepless nights. What if her man never returned? What would happen to her and her child?

It was well that she did not know of the fevers and of the women lurking in the new country waiting for the chance to pounce on the unsuspecting. Like the rattlesnake that lay in wait by the water of the diggings, both were deadly. Typhoid in its various forms was omnipresent in all the mining camps. Malaria was epidemic in the camps close to the floor of the interior valleys. Multiple forms of food poisoning lurked in the kitchen of every boarding house and of every hotel.

While the fevers were dangerous, and thousands were to die from them during the first years of the Gold Rush, the danger from the women was many times greater. Excluding the women of the Mexican ranchers and the wives and daughters of the few American government officials and a scattering of Yankee traders at the seaports, ninety-five percent of all the women in California during the first two years of the Rush were saloon girls. They consorted with men infected by every venereal disease known. In particular, they were almost sure to be infected with the most virulent strains of gonorrhea and syphilis, acquired by contact with sailors off the ships in the trade with the coastal cities of China, hot in their pursuit of pleasure after long months at sea.

Naturally these women followed the miners to the richest camps. Even if by chance they had escaped infection, they were still more deadly than the most venomous of snakes. If they could not get all of the contents of the miner's poke by doing what came naturally, they put drugs in his drinks. If he was lucky he awoke a poorer and a wiser man. If a woman put too much laudanum in his whiskey, he died in his sleep of a "heart attack"! If the poison was not available, a sharp knife between the fifth and sixth ribs of the drunken sleeper had the desired effect. "After all, a woman had to protect her honor!" So protesting, she was relatively safe. In all the violent history of early California, only one woman was ever executed for murder. That was a poor Mexican girl who knifed her lover in a drunken brawl. She paid for her proficiency with the dirk by dangling at the end of a rope beneath the bridge spanning the Yuba River at Downieville.

Mary was sure that Michael would resist the California women for a time. But after a year of ardent lovemaking following their marriage, his new life of celibacy might not be bearable. Who knew what a desperate man might do so far from home?

Not even the brightness of the October morning or the flame of the frost-seared sugar maples relieved Mary's depression. She sat at the kitchen table, her chin cupped in her hands, fighting to keep back the tears of self-pity. Suddenly she was startled to hear the door behind her being pushed cautiously open.

The Sullivans always knocked before they came in, even though they worked for her. She instinctively thought of the gun that she had kept loaded and primed since Michael had left. Her heart sank and she felt a tightness in her throat when she remembered that it was in the bedroom. The first time that she might need it, and it was not at hand!

Then in a dreamlike trance she listened to a familiar voice, speaking in the dialect of the Irish countryside:

"Mary, me darlin', could ye be sparin' a weary travelin' mon a wee kiss?"

Unbelieving, she sat for an instant. Then with a little squeal of delight, she spun around and threw herself into the arms of her grinning man.

After the rush of the greeting, he pushed her away. "Well, let's see him!"

She was tempted to punish him for arriving unannounced by telling him that the "him" was a "her." But she was too proud of her son to resort to the deception. She took his arm and led him into the bedroom, where the baby lay cooing, content with the world after his breakfast of milk and gruel.

"You'll love him, Michael. He's so sweet and good."

She had completely forgotten her sore breast. All that really mattered was that her man was home, suntanned and healthy!

She took little Joe out of his crib and handed him to his father.

"Here," she said. "Maybe you brought some gold back from California. But what I gave you is worth much more than all the treasure you could have carried to me."

He held the baby for a moment, instinctively looking for and finding the "Irish look." Then he put him down and looked long and hard at his wife. She seemed to be in good health. In particular he noted the slimness. She presented a far different silhouette than she had when he had left her almost a year before.

"You've lost some weight since I saw you last."

"Well, at least I've got something to show for it!" She laughed, and her face flushed as she made the flippant reply. She knew very well what was on his mind.

"I'm not sure that I like you so slim. The other way looks better to me." A boyish grin came over his face before he added, "And I know damned well how I can remedy the situation!" "Oh, Michael!" was all she could say before he swept her off her feet and drew her gently to the bed.

She made no protest. She too knew what to do about the slimness he did not approve of!

Only ninety days were allowed to do all the things that had to be done before the McGuires were aboard the steamer bound for Panama.

Michael had reserved space aboard the Pacific mail steamer scheduled to sail from Panama City on or about March 1, 1850. Not to have done so would have been sheer madness. No sane man would knowingly take his family across the Isthmus without means of whisking them away from the disease-spreading insects and the tainted water of the tropics. Very few women and practically no children who were forced to wait their turn for deck space from Panama north escaped some form of infection. In a high percentage of the cases the malaise proved to be fatal.

Michael had also reserved and paid for passage on the Colón-bound steamer, as well as arranging for quick passage across the Isthmus. Ninety days was not too long to sell the farm and dispose of all the things they had accumulated during the time that they had lived and worked there.

Only necessary clothing and materials for the care of the baby made up their baggage. Across Panama, they must travel light. It would not do to slow up their progress for an instant by taking anything but the barest of necessities. Michael knew that by the time he returned to California, clipper ships would have rounded the Horn with most of the goods so badly needed on the coast and with some of the luxuries demanded by the argonauts. The prices would be high, but not too high in camparison to the cost of being delayed in Panama.

Little Joe was covered by clothing, so that he did not get bitten by the insects during the trip. Michael's beard and the leatherlike quality of his exposed skin gave him the protection he needed, but Mary's fair and tender skin offered a choice target. Two weeks out of Panama she began to suffer from recurring chills and fevers. The ship's doctor recognized malaria. Fortunately, she had escaped the far more dangerous yellow fever.

Not until they had reached the cool spring weather of the Sierras did the symptoms of the malignant infection subside, but during the heat of the summer for years thereafter she suffered periodic chills followed by the dread fevers. Over the years, the lingering infection, coupled with Michael's ability to insure that "plump look," sometimes caused her to wonder if it had all been worthwhile.

Mostly, however, she was far too busy with her ever-expanding family to give much thought to her own troubles. She had to see that each was fed and clothed. They had to be given the religious training the Church demanded, and she also had to see that each was given the education she knew he must have; not a small task considering the number of things that were of far more interest to growing boys in the developing mining camps of California.

To be sure that each child would get all the education he or she desired, Mary had one hard and fast rule. At the birth of each new addition to the "clan," Michael was sent to town to deposit $1,000 in the most reliable bank. This was sacred money to be used only for the education of the newborn. She took a small amount of sadistic pleasure as she watched Michael work the extra hours to recover the additional sixty ounces of gold needed to make that deposit. She well knew that she had been as much to blame as he for their bed habits. But this progressively became a little much. Ten children between 1848 and 1878! Certainly, the admonition in Genesis, "Go ye forth and populate the earth," was followed with religious fervor by the McGuires!

Sad to relate, the last of the $1,000 deposits had been drawing interest in the bank but six months when poor management caused the bank to fail. The entire amount was lost!

Undaunted, Michael called the family together and assured them that their real educational funds were in his unfailing bank, the gravel of the McGuire Mine. Those who wished to continue their education beyond the local Union Hill School could still carry out their plans. Only Jim and Tom of the boys, and Minnie of the girls, took advantage of the offer. Sarah and Lucy married early. The other boys became too engrossed in mining and in making money in other fields to continue school beyond the sixth grade. Their reasoning was what good was book learning when they could work a few years, learning all there was to know about mining, then go out, find a mine of their own, and get rich working it?

5

Back to the Mines

McGuire had embarked on the riverboat at Marysville on September 1, 1849. A week later he stood on the deck of the Panama-bound steamer and watched Tamalpias on the north, and the sand dunes on the south, disappear as the ship dipped her bow into the long swells of the Pacific beyond the Golden Gate.

On April 10, 1850, he helped Mary as she carried the baby down the gangplank to the riverside dock, which had been built on the north bank of the Yuba River. This was at almost the exact spot where he had been rowed ashore the year before, almost to the day.

During the entire westward voyage he had been a celebrity aboard the ships on which they sailed. Here was a living, breathing miner—one who had really lived and worked in the fabulous land of California. He actually had chunks of gold that he had dug out of the stream beds with his own hands to prove that he knew whereof he spoke! Further, if that were not enough to prove that he had a right to speak of the mines, he carelessly tossed a small handful of gold dust onto the sands of the beach at Panama and demonstrated the use of the gold pan. So sure was he of his ability to recover all the "dust" that he did not bother to weigh the gold before he made the demonstration. He knew he would recover it all.

Only the captain of the ship rated more attention and respect from the men bound for the mines. To be able to talk to either of these "demigods" was an experience of which a passenger could boast for days.

Liquor was forbidden aboard the ships. Experience had taught that a ship crowded with men till it was difficult to find deck space to spread a blanket for sleeping was no place for a man in his cups. It was too easy to toss him overboard, and the temptation was great to do just that if he happened to occupy a sheltered place with his belongings.

But of course there was liquor. It came aboard in flasks smuggled and sold by the crew. Mostly the captain looked the other way. How else was he to get stokers and deckhands? Unless they could make a few hundred extra dollars on each trip, they merely took off for the mines.

Even before his newfound notoriety, Michael had stood out in crowds. His tall, solid frame made him a man to be reckoned with. His Irish charm and his Irish wit had always attracted attention. Now he could find almost no time for his family. Mary had a quick remedy for this.

For the third night in succession he had come into their cabin well after midnight, reeking of cheap whiskey the men had almost forced on him to get him to talk more of the mines.

"That will be all of this, Michael McGuire," she had said in a voice that cut through the haze of the alcohol. "I'll stand for no more of this foolishness. If you are half the man I thought I married, you'll get down on your knees right now and thank the good Lord for leading you to the riches. And don't you be thinking that he had nothing to do with it. You're a smart man, Michael McGuire, else I'd have had nothing to do with the likes of you, but you're not that smart. 'Twas your faith in our dear Lord that led Him to lead you to all that gold. And while you're about it, it might do your fickle soul good to thank our dear Jesus for allowing you to have a tolerant wife who was willing to allow you to go traipsing all over the world looking for gold just when she was about to present you with a fine son! A son that you don't seem to appreciate, I might add!"

Michael slumped in the bunk bed. He knew that she was right. He had made a fool of himself. He wanted to apologize, but the liquor would not let the words come. He tried to hold her, but he smelled too much of sweat and of cheap liquor. She pushed him away—something she had never done before.

He awoke the following morning a contrite man. He said nothing, but he made a point of carrying little Joe out onto the deck to display him to the admirers, and to give him the fresh air and the sunshine he needed. When Mary was stricken with malaria, he somehow blamed himself for her troubles.

"Dear God," he prayed, "punish me! 'Twas I who sinned. Relieve that sweet soul of her misery. Let me be stricken in her place."

During her chills and her fever, he was constantly at her side. The crowded decks saw very little of him during those trying days.

As if in answer to his prayers, the ship left the tropical waters at the latitude off the California coast opposite Point McGoo. There it entered the chill waters of the Alaskan Current. The sudden lowering of the temperature performed a miracle. Thereafter, so long as the weather remained cool, Mary suffered no more attacks.

The day after the crossing into the cool fog that shrouded the cool water, she was able to stand on deck with Michael and watch the rays of the setting sun reflected from the whitewashed adobe walls of the buildings of Monterey. The following morning as the fog lifted, she looked in wonderment as the entrance of San Francisco Bay slashed between the heretofore solid battlement of hills and mountains that make up most of the coast of California from Mexico to Oregon.

The prevailing westerlies and the incoming tide swept the steamer at a smart clip across the blue of the yet-unpolluted bay toward the long rampart of green hills on the Contra Costa shores.

Suddenly, as the ship slid past Telegraph Hill, Mary and every other passenger on deck gasped in amazement at the sight that lay before them.

Michael had told of the fifty ships that had been abandoned to rot on the mud flats off Montgomery Street. Now there were a hundred and fifty! Even he had not been prepared for the enormity of the waste. The crowded decks, which had been covered by cheering men, suddenly carried only awestruck passengers, each sobered by the sight of the real evidence of the mad rush to get to the hills to gather the gold before it had been picked clean by the throngs its magnetism had attracted—each man suddenly having it forced upon his consciousness that he indeed was a part of the great adventure—each secretly beginning to plot how best he could get ahead of his shipmates once the ship had docked.

Already the enterprising merchants of the town had scuttled a chain of abandoned ships leading a thousand feet out into the bay. With redwood planking they had bridged the space between decks. Now the newly arrived ships were busily unloading their cargoes directly onto the improvised wharf. The Pacific mail steamer, being under government contract, and carrying mail, had priority. Space was cleared for her immediately. A thousand people stood on the dock to greet the new arrivals, but mainly they were there to be the first to get copies of Eastern newspapers and important letters which had been sent by couriers. Ten dollars was the going price for a thirty-day-old paper, and the special letter charge was five dollars. The papers and the special letters were sent ashore ahead of even the first-class passengers.

Two days had to pass before a boat would leave for upriver. The McGuires were forced to seek housing. This they found on one of the scuttled ships. An enterprising innkeeper had refitted the interior of a scuttled clipper ship making it into a hotel, complete with bar and dining room.*

It is questionable who was the more impressed, Michael or Mary, by the small city that had suddenly appeared on the northeastern shore of the peninsula, which enclosed the southern arm of the bay. Michael remembered it as first a deserted village

---

*One hundred years later the youngest of the McGuires, Michael Junior, descended the stairs into the basement of a ten-story office building on Montgomery Street. There he was served food and drink in the very room where his parents had eaten their first meal in California! Not one person in a thousand who patronizes this unique restaurant realizes that the bar is a part of the captain's cabin of a proud clipper ship, now buried by the debris that pushed the waterfront more than a thousand feet north to the embarcado.

in the spring of 1849, then as a mushrooming town of about five hundred souls when he embarked for Panama in the fall of that same year. Now, only six months later, a great city was clearly in the making.

Already, hundreds of buildings were occupied by infant business firms. A thousand houses of various types and in various stages of construction were scattered along the rocky hillsides and across the sandy flats. Rough houses were being rushed to completion as fast as materials could be found and labor be hired, to house the two thousand or more people living here in tents. Even these when completed would not suffice to shelter the multitudes who had deserted the ships in the harbor, or had quit the mines, either in disgust at not having found gold to be picked up along the stream beds, or because they had picked it up and had found the action in the camps too tame. Instinctively, they had rushed to the nearest seaport, where past experience told them that liquor and women were always to be found in unlimited quantities by those who had the price.

Mary saw only the mass of people congregated here to form a cosmopolitan city. For the first time she heard and failed to understand the languages being spoken. Naturally, English, from "Down East Yankee" to British Cockney, predominated. But here on some streets strange foreign sounds were to be heard: mostly Spanish, as the Mexicans, the Chilianos, and the natives of a dozen other South and Central American countries mixed with the few native Californians, aliens and lost in their own country.

In the next block the soft musical sounds of the Latins might suddenly change to the singsong of the Cantonese, as the business establishments changed from Mexican stores festooned with brightly colored corn, and with the brilliance of red and green peppers, to shops selling dried octopus, cuttlefish, pressed duck, hundred-year-old eggs, and the ingredients for bird's nest soup!

Mary learned quickly to identify the strange people by their costumes, or by the words and phrases, which shortly were identifiable. But the workers on the dock mystified her. They were a brown-skinned people of magnificent physical proportions.

They spoke a language that seemed but a succession of vowels. Not a single syllable could she recognize.

Michael explained that these were the Kanakas, a name given to the natives of the Sandwich Islands. Numbers of them had been in California before gold was discovered. Some had deserted from the whalers when they had put in to shore to replenish their supplies of fuel and water. Some had been brought over by Captain Sutter, the men to work at his fort on the American River, and some of the women at least, to serve him personally. But mostly they had made up the crews of the ships that made the regular run from the Islands to the Bay of San Francisco. Once ships from all over the world.

Once away from the water, however, they were lost. Very few of them ever did any serious mining. Almost without exception they left the hills and found work on the riverboats, or on the docks loading and unloading the ships. Some had established small colonies on the banks of the Sacramento River. There they made an easy living netting the limitless migrating salmon. They sold the succulent fish to the forty-niners, who were sick unto death of their diet of beans, sowbelly, and stringy beef. The Kanakas would make up most of the crew of the river packet that would take the McGuires up the Sacramento and the Feather rivers to Marysville.

Two days in the crush of humanity, and in wading through the mud of what passed for streets in San Francisco, was enough for the McGuires. They had been used to the clean country air of the farm. They resented being surrounded by the smells that must develop when humans are packed into such small areas, and where there were no sanitation facilities other than the ever-present outhouses at the rear of each house and of each business establishment, or, as here in the water-oriented community, suspended over the sides of the grounded ships, where the incoming tides washed the sewage ashore, to be carried out to sea—it was hoped!—when the tide next turned.

The McGuires breathed a sigh of relief when the little steamer chugged away from the landing at California and Montgomery Streets.

The early morning sun was just beginning to dispel the night-generated fog, revealing the imaginary figure of a reclining woman silhouetted along the southern slopes of Mount Tamalpais. To the east the ranchland of the Costas and the Peraltas stretched back indefinitely into the hills, which formed the picturesque backdrop for the panorama of the bay. To the north the hills tapered gently to the gap of the Straights of Carquenez, where the Pacific Tides made navigation a hazard, and through which the cooling sea breezes often turned to near hurricane velocity when the days were hot in the interior valleys.

After an hour they passed Red Rock and came out on the gentler surface of San Pablo Bay. A fellow passenger pointed out the wooded canyons on the slopes of Tamalpais, and told outrageous lies of the trees fifteen to twenty feet in diameter growing there, trees so large that they defied the efforts of men to cut them down for lumber. Michael walked away in disgust. Why, he had sugar and ponderosa pine on his property four to five feet thick at their base. These, he knew, must be the largest trees in the world! Trees four times that large? Impossible!

Just a year before, as he and the other passengers had helped the Kanakas add to the power of the tiny steam engine and row upriver against the current of the flooded rivers and the ebb of the tides, he had seen thousands of Mexican cattle grazing on the open grassy hillsides. He had thought that never had he seen more beautiful pasture land. Now the hills stood unpopulated. Lush grass stood belly-high to a horse, but not an animal was in sight, growing fat on the abundance. To his inquiry, the engineer-pilot of the boat told him that the cattle had all been slaughtered to feed the great influx of gold-seekers. Mostly they had been stolen. Often the Mexican owners had stood helplessly by and watched the butchery! To the Americans, these cattle on the open range had no owner and were as free as the elk and the deer they had also killed until they had become practically extinct.

Michael was soon to see that he was correct. Where, before, countless herds of elk crowded the riverbanks and fed in the tule marshes of the delta region at the mating of the Sacramento and the San Joaquin rivers, now only the untold thousands of waterfowl, those which had opted to stay and nest on the winter feeding grounds rather than migrate to the lakes, the swamps, and the tundra of the Canadian north, remained to tell the traveler that this was indeed a land of vast productivity. Even the grizzlies were no longer in evidence, pushed out of their natural habitat by the one other animal with which they could not cope—the hunter with his rifle.

The spring rains and the melting winter snows of the mountains had put the rivers at their annual flood stage. The little steamer rode the crest of the flood, well above the normal banks of the stream. Mary gasped in astonishment at the panorama that unfolded as they rounded each new meander. As far as the eye could see, high grasses bowed to the gentle breeze. On the stretches of the less fertile soils, golden California poppies carpeted the ground: golden to see at close range, but, by some strange chance of pigmentation, shaded to the most dazzling of reds as the distance from the beholder increased. Interspersed with the poppies were acres of blue lupines. Fairer fields would be hard to imagine.

But the sight that brought oohs and ahs from even the most hardened of the travelers was the great panorama of the snow-covered Sierra Nevada Mountains stretching from horizon to horizon to the east, the milk-white peaks etched against the azure of the Nevada sky. They stood above the dark green of the forests and the lighter greens of the brush and grasslands below the timber line. The effect was that of a well-filled bodice surmounting a skirt of Irish tartan woven from wool of intermingling shades of green.

Even the river men feasted their eyes on the sight. They knew that this was a vision that was only a springtime phenomenon. Summer haze would block the view after the middle of May. Then, when the winter snows arrived to carpet the hills once more, the everlasting valley fogs would block the sight from their eyes. When the fog dissipated, the peaks were most often blanketed by the stormclouds of the Pacific storms following one another down out of the Gulf of Alaska at weekly intervals during the winter months.*

Mary was speechless when Michael told her of Bidwell's advice to buy several thousand acres of the rich bottom land from one of the Spanish land grants, and become a landed "baron" in the new Territory, an area that very shortly must become a state. Her private thought was that the California pioneer had most probably been right, but she was too wise to criticize his choice. Her only comment was "Perhaps when all the gold is mined, we should take Mr. Bidwells' advice."

His reply was to tell her, "I'll take you to Marysville some day in July or in August. One day of that fiery furnace, breathing the dust, and being eaten by the clouds of mosquitoes will make you realize just what a smart husband you have. Our mine is above the haze and the heat of the summer and above the fogs of the winter months. It is also below all but an occasional snowfall. Mary, my darling, you'll love it there in the trees with a nice little brook running right by your kitchen door. And what a place to raise our children!" He smiled as he patted her on the stomach, which he knew would soon begin to swell once more.

Sacramento was a disaster. Just as the river men had predicted, the winter floods had covered the entire town. The swirling muddy water had reached to the second floor of the buildings that had an upper story. These, and the few other buildings that had not been carried away, now stood at grotesque angles as first one side, then another had been undermined. The soft silt and the river sands had offered little or no resistance to the sucking currents of the river.

Captain Sutter was in a mood of great glee! He had told the squatters along the river bank that they had best spend a little money to buy higher ground near his fort if they wished to start

---

*The stormclouds are checked in their easterly flight by the rising mountain barrier, where their moisture is squeezed out and deposited in great banks of snow, before they are allowed to continue on their way across the thirsty lands of the Great Basin.

a town. Now, instead of offering to help the unfortunate, he had doubled the price of the land that would be safe from the floods. In doing this he had antagonized the entire business community.

The businessmen considered his actions blackmail. They voted to boycott his land sale scheme. Instead they would spend the money necessary to build levees to hold back the river.

For a few years the artificial banks held, but soon the first of the thirty cubic miles of debris from the hydraulic mines began to choke the river channels. Then nothing could stop the spreading of the floodwaters across the entire valley.

The docks, of course, had to be built by the riverside. But greed prompted the building and the rebuilding of the hotels, the saloons with their upstairs rooms for the girls, and the honest mercantile stores as close to the river front as possible. Each owner had to be the first in line to extract the gold from the pockets of the miners coming down the rivers—gold from men who had spent long months isolated in the mountains, grubbing in the mud, eating beans and sowbelly, sleeping under soggy blankets spread on piles of brush in lieu of a mattress. Here there was whiskey to dull the memory of the torment. Here were women to relieve that awful longing and drive that has pushed every virile man since time began. Here they were to be had for a price, and the price was exactly what most of the men coming out of the hills had! Here too was food—food the likes of which a man could only dream of before he had found gold. He could not wait. Half a mile was too far. He had arrived in paradise. He must begin to enjoy it now! The businessmen were there to accommodate him. They crowded the river banks with the accommodations the miners sought.

But when the McGuires arrived at Sacramento there was not only "no room in the inn," there was no inn! They spent a restless night aboard the riverboat.

Michael had anticipated seeing Captain Sutter again and showing Mary the wonders of the fort the Swiss adventurer had built here in the wilderness long before gold had ever been dreamed of. They were unable to land. So they had to be content to listen to the stories of his successes.

By now, Sutter had to be considered a very rich man. Had he been able to collect royalties from the gold mined on his holdings, as did General Frémont from his Mariposa Spanish Land grant, he would have been the richest private citizen in the world. Only the absolute monarchs of the world could have owned more. No amount of riotous living and unwise business ventures could have dented his vast fortune. Still, his land holdings, even without the gold, and without the herds of cattle and flocks of sheep and swine, must surely be worth in excess of $20,000,000. Few men could boast of as much!

As soon as light permitted the pilot to keep to the main channel and to dodge the snags and dislodged trees borne by the floodwaters, the little paddle wheel steamer continued upstream.

Again Michael was struck by the absence of game and of cattle on the high ground. Once more the pilot told of the game being hunted to near extinction. But here the cattle had been under the watchful eyes of Sutter's herders. That did not prove to be sufficient. The guards could not watch all the cattle all the time. Gangs of cattle rustlers ran off with Sutter's cattle, butchered them in secluded spots, and actually sold the meat back to the hungry people at the fort. The stock the rustlers missed the squatters appropriated for the beginnings of their own herds.

Only at Sutter"s Hock Farm, ten miles below Marysville, was there any evidence of ranching. There the captain had stationed his most trusted Kanakas in a vain attempt to save some of his herds, and to try to continue to raise grain for his mill at Natomas. Eventually, this too was lost to the creditors who crashed down on the overextended millionaire when the first crack in his empire appeared. All his 200,000 acres of rich land went to creditors who held a few thousand dollars worth of his notes. His cattle, horses, hogs, and sheep were stolen by the gold-mad men who poured down out of the hills, convinced that, as Americans, they were free to take anything formerly owned by the "foreigners."

The fact that the Treaty of Hidalgo, which gave California to the United States, had guaranteed all residents of the territory full citizenship and had warranted the title to all property they had owned at that time, meant nothing to the argonauts. "This was America now, and, by God, no heathen foreigner was going to keep all those riches! Who won the war anyway?"

The courts offered no protection. It was twenty years before the United States Supreme Court ruled in favor of the original owners. Meanwhile, only a few lived to repossess their land. All their other wealth had long since been dissipated. Sutter died a pauper in a Pennsylvania rooming house!

John Bidwell was one of the few who managed to retain his land and his personal property. He organized a small army. His forces were more formidable than the organized gangs of cutthroats and rustlers who terrorized the foothills and the valley. His patrols moved the squatters off before they could establish any claim to the land on which they had tried to settle. His men had orders to shoot first, then ask the questions. It was remarkable how fast his reputation spread over the thinly populated country. Ten rustlers were either shot or hanged early in the winter of 1849-50. Thereafter his cattle were relatively safe.

Like Sacramento, Marysville was mostly under water. A dock had been built at the foot of Second Street. This was connected by an elevated walkway to the few remaining buildings situated on the higher ground. The passengers were able to make their way safely to the business establishments without being ferried ashore in small boats.

The team and wagon that had been purchased for the McGuires was ready and waiting. Some few pieces of furniture had been obtained, but mostly Mary would just have to make do. They wasted no time in town, but immediately joined the procession of passengers from the boat. There were no accommodations in town for anyone. The newcomers were forced to make their way to even higher ground, where they might safely camp.

In the preceding fall the road had been ankle-deep in dust. Now it was hub-deep in mud. Progress was painful and slow, but they did reach an area far enough from the river to escape the voracious mosquitoes. There they camped and spent their first night in the strange new world.

Away from the river, the road crossed a plain of compacted ancient river gravel. This they followed across the valley to the first oak-studded foothills. Except for an occasional swale, no more mud caused their team to labor with even the lightly loaded wagon. Thereafter only the steep pitches of the hills slowed their progress.

The original mine trails had followed the rivers and the creeks, but these in a short time always gave way to the easier routes along the ridges that lay between the drainage basins of the streams. In the foothills of the Sierras, the average grade was one hundred feet to the mile. This was an easy pull. But road building was not always that simple. The country was broken. Valleys of almost flat land might stretch for several miles; then a ridge had to be climbed. Here the narrow wagon road twisted and turned to gain the needed elevation. Here the horses labored, often progressing only a few hundred yards before being forced to rest.

These were the roads where, twenty years later, the "jerk line" teams of ten horses or mules, hauling two or more wagons, were preceded by a trained shepherd dog, which, being met by a downgrade-bound wagon, "told" the driver that an upgrade team was less than a quarter mile behind. The downgrade wagon had to find a place to pull off the road to allow the laboring team to pass.

As yet there was not that much traffic, so the McGuires climbed the grade through the foothills into Penn Valley with no delays. There they camped during the second night. Squirrel Creek offered water. Its banks grew thick with forage for the horses. Normally the stream ran clear at this time of the year. Michael had expected to find it so now. Instead it was red with the iron-stained mud from the hillsides above. This was not due to a recent storm, but to the activities of two hundred miners working sixteen to eighteen hours each day to wash gold from the stream banks, rushing to get all the gold possible while there was still enough water in the small tributary streams to separate the gold from the gravel.

Michael had heard of the new device called the "rocker," which had vastly speeded up the work of the miners. On Squirrel Creek, he saw one in operation for the first time.

Roughly, the rocker, or "cradle," was a device somewhat like a baby's rocker with holes bored through its bottom (the rocker's, not the baby's). Ore-bearing gravel was shoveled into the space normally occupied by the baby. Water was poured over it while the operator moved the device back and forth with a jerking motion. The fine material, which contained all the gold except the most unusual nugget, was washed through the perforations (later a screen) into a gold pan and was washed in the normal manner. The coarse material was discarded and the rocker filled again.

Almost immediately an improvement was made. Someone placed the curved rockers on a sloping board or platform on which he had nailed half-inch cleats. The heavy gold was trapped back of these. The valueless material was washed away by the excess water. Now even less panning had to be done.

Michael saw the advantage of the new machine immediately. With a pan alone, he could work about half a yard of gravel per day. Now, if water was readily available, he could wash two full yards. Further he saw that the miner's hands need not be immersed in the cold water during most of the mining process. Then, too, where it would formerly not have been profitable to work more than one-tenth of the area of his claim, now fully half of it could be washed. Best of all, the work would be far less arduous.

The following morning he urged the horses to renewed efforts in his haste to cross the final divide between Squirrel Creek and Boston Ravine. Near the top of that grade they passed within a hundred yards of the hillside where a few months later nuggets were found in the roots of clumps of dried grass being gathered for tinder. The lucky finders were en route to Marysville. Needless to say they got no farther! Instead, a new town known as Rough and Ready was founded by the miners, who were admirers of Zachary Taylor. Ten years later, these same people disagreed with Lincoln's Civil War policies. They seceded from the Union and formed their own republic, complete with their own president and congress.

Fortunately no one took them seriously. As long as they continued to pay their taxes to Nevada County, nothing was done about their disloyalty. In time the whole thing was forgotten; then it was resurrected by local historians looking for a "cause." In 1957, the "Territory" was formally readmitted into Nevada County by resolution of the Board of Supervisors. Once more the dry gulch, with its semighost town became part of the United States!

No road had yet been built up Little Wolf Creek from Lamarque's to the claim, but Michael had little trouble making his way with the wagon up the ridge north of the creek. The hillside stood canopied by massive pine and cedar trees. No underbrush could develop in the dense shade to impede their progress. The area was almost parklike, shaded by 150-foot trees, and carpeted by centuries of accumulated pine needles. Only an occasional rock outcropping or a fallen tree had to be skirted to gain the level area, which had come to be known as "McGuire Flat."

At Boston Ravine, Lamarque already had an improved rocker for sale. This new machine had the cleated platform mounted between the curved rocker boards. Now it too moved with the rocker. As the fine material worked through the perforations it fell on the moving cleated board, and the heavy gold was separated with still greater efficiency. Now fully ninety-five percent of the panning was eliminated. The device could be operated for a full day before the material from the upper side of the riffles need be scraped out and panned. Of course the tailings from the rocker were still run over rough rocks and rubble before they were allowed to reenter the stream and be lost. But that area had only to be "cleaned up" at the end of each mining season to recover the "flour gold" too light to be trapped by the rocker.

While there was still sufficient water in the stream, Michael worked with his new tools on the richest part of the claims. They lived or "camped" in the lean-to he had built the preceding year. When the stream dwindled to a trickle, he first dug a well to assure a constant drinking water supply during the dry season, then he set about building a cabin. They had to have shelter for the coming winter.

Lumber was expensive, but it was available. One of the forty-niners, coming across the plains, had managed to get through with the essential parts of a sawmill. A waterwheel on Wolf

Creek supplied the needed power. In the east, the mill operator would have been glad to get $10 to $15 per thousand board feet for his product. Here the going price was $100! In addition, the prospective purchaser had to deliver to the mill an equivalent amount of lumber in the form of saw logs. This presented a problem. Even when a man was equipped with the proper tools for felling the giants of the forest, the resulting logs were so huge that no wagon would stand their weight. For a time at least, the trees to be cut stood on the slopes of the hills immediately above the mill. The logs could be skidded down the steep hillsides.

Men who had not found gold, or whose claims could not be worked during the dry summer, were now busy cutting the timber, sliding the logs to the mill, and delivering the lumber to the new town of Grass Valley, which was building just half a mile upstream from Boston Ravine.

Other out-of-work miners were now available to do any number of things. During that first summer following the arrival of the first of the mass of forty-niners wages fell from an ounce of gold per day to $5. With skilled help at this wage available, the McGuire cabin was completed long before the winter storms arrived.

Released from mining and from house building, Michael went to work clearing the bench to the north and east of the mining area. Prospecting had shown that there was no gold here. It would be the garden and the orchard. Later they would build a fine "New England" farmhouse for the growing family. Eventually, some twelve acres were cleared and farmed. The famous Gilette nursery was established in Nevada City in the mid-1850s. From there Michael obtained the trees he planted in 1860. Although they have not been irrigated, pruned, or sprayed for over fifty years, many of these same trees are still producing apples and pears in the 1970s. The farmhouse continued to be occupied until 1948. Then it was declared a public nuisance and a fire hazard and had to be demolished. A series of "poor renters" had ruined it.

6

Gold in the Rocks!

As did most of the other miners, McGuire speculated from time to time about the source of the gold in the gravel. That it had been carried to its present location by running water was obvious. But why, for example, did some streams carry no gold while just over a ridge the neighboring stream had rich benches and bars? Why did some streams give up large nuggets along their lower reaches, then contain nothing above a given point? And why did the streams that did carry gold, almost without exception, carry very little gold above 3,500 feet in elevation in the north, and above 1,500 feet at the southern limits of the "Mother Lode"?

The religious said, "God put it there. We should not question His plan!" More commonly, the superstitious said, "Gold is where you find it. If you are lucky you'll get it. If not, no matter how hard you try, you'll miss it every time. All anyone can do is to try this luck to see if fate will be kind to him!"

McGuire was inclined to side with the religious. All his early training in the Church and in the Church-run schools had been firm in the teaching of the Divine Will. One must accept such things on faith. It did not occur to him to question. God had been good to him. He had led him straight to the gold mine. He had provided him with a most beautiful and desirable wife. He had already given him one son and another was on the way. Surely it would be followed by many more. Who was he to question God's will?

His early Church training was not shaken in the slightest when Agassiz, and other geologists demonstrated that the gold

57

in the streams had come as the result of millions of years of the erosion of whole mountains, and was the result of the concentration of the heavy metal in the gravel, and especially in the gravel close to the bedrock of the stream beds.

Long before the geologists arrived, the problem was solved in part by George McKnight's discovery of gold in the quartz rock he had picked up on "Gold Hill," just a quarter mile from Lamarque's saloon at Boston Ravine.

McGuire was sure that God had directed the Scotsman to the exact spot and he had put him in the black mood that had controlled his actions. Why the Lord would pick a heretic Presbyterian to carry out this most important mission Michael could never understand. He had been taught to accept such things on faith alone. He assumed that the Church leaders would be able to explain. But that was their business. He most probably would not understand, should they attempt to enlighten the world on such matters.

McKnight, in October, 1850, was placer mining on Rhode Island Ravine. The fall rains had not yet arrived, so the gravel he and the other miners uncovered and scraped off the bedrock could not be washed at the claims. Instead, it was carried across the shoulder of a small hill to Wolf Creek, which carried a good "head" of water at all times of the year. There at the end of each day of hard digging, the miners congregated on the banks of the stream and vied with one another in a panning contest, each striving to be the first to finish the hundred pounds of gravel they had carried here, and each trying to pan the material with the least possible loss of value.

Some days a lucky miner might get a full ounce of gold. Usually, their take was nearer a quarter as much. With gold bringing only $15 an ounce at the saloon, and food selling for a dollar or more per pound, the miners were not doing too well.

No wonder McKnight was disgusted with his fate. Instead of getting rich, he was lucky to be making enough to buy beans and fatty salted pork. No wonder then, when he stubbed his toe on a rock that protruded from the side of the footpath he was following to the water, he uttered some words not recommended for

Sunday school, and kicked at the offending stone. A portion of the outcropping broke free and rolled ahead of him along the path. As it moved, the rays of the late afternoon sun reflected from the freshly broken surface of a bright yellow metal!

Most miners had found quartz pebbles and even a few irregular pieces of broken quartz in which they noticed specks of embedded gold. A few had even broken the rock into small pieces and had panned out the liberated gold. But no one had as yet speculated that the gold in the streams had come from just such rocks as these, which had originally been embedded in the crust of the earth.

McKnight's find was unique. First, the rock he picked up after his toe had stopped hurting was noticeably heavier than the stream gravel. This he quickly surmised was due to the weight of the metal it contained. Second, it was unique because he knew the exact source of the specimen he had picked up. All the other rocks found by the miners had been carried by running water to the location where they had been found. There was just no possibility of anyone's ever tracing them back to their origin.

McKnight let the sack of gravel he had been carrying lie by the side of the path. He ran all the way to his cabin. In great excitement he picked up a hammer and a gold pan. Then he ran the remaining distance to the creek bank, to a spot where he would be out of sight of the other miners, and where he knew there was a large flat rock. He placed the piece of quartz on the surface of the rock and pounded it into a fine sand. This he swept into his pan, dipped it into the water, and, with a few skilled motions learned in many hours of prospecting, he separated the quartz sand from the gold. He hardly dared hope that it really was gold. If it was, he had recovered as much in just a few minutes of easy work as he had been able to pan out of the creek in all of the preceding month!

Lamarque looked long and hard at the bright shiny gold McKnight used to pay for his evening shot of whiskey. He put a piece between his teeth and bit down hard. It was malleable. He put some on the gold scales. It weighed out, so he nodded and accepted the proffered payment.

McKnight could hardly hide his elation. Lamarque was the local gold buyer. He was supposed to be an expert on such things. If he accepted it, the material must be gold, or at least it was a substance that would pass for gold. He was not really concerned as to which.

In the morning he did not work his placer claim. Instead, he got his pick and shovel from the claim before the neighboring miners had arrived. He then returned to the spot on the trail where he had dropped the sack of gravel the evening before. In only a few minutes he exposed a four-inch layer of whitish quartz rock running in a north-south direction and "dipping" into the red dirt at an angle of about forty degrees from the horizontal. Most wonderful of all, the surface of the rock from which he had broken the two-pound sample the evening before showed more of the embedded metal!

Quickly, he broke off twenty pounds of the exposed mineral and carried it down to the creek. Within two hours he crushed and panned his find. The crushed rock panned out almost two pounds of gold—more gold than he had seen in any one man's possession since he had arrived in the mines!

He ran to the store and bar. Lamarque examined the metal once more, this time, as Sutter had done when Marshall brought in the first sample of the heavy yellow metal from the millrace, he tested it with nitric acid from his medical kit. The metal was not affected by the acid. Therefore it must be GOLD!

McKnight knew that his new find would be safe. His mining tools were on the location. The unwritten law of the mines would protect his interest for a full thirty days; so he went on one glorious drunk.

Why not? He had found the source of all the gold in California! Suddenly he was a millionaire! He had wealth beyond his wildest dreams!

Of course it did not turn out that way. History does not record what became of McKnight. Most probably, he took out a few thousand dollars in gold. He then returned to Ohio or to Indiana, bought a farm, and spent the rest of his life raising corn, hogs, and children!

Gold in quartz was, and is, most unpredictable. The "pocket," or "chimney," of "highgrade ore" that McKnight had uncovered went only a few feet into the earth, then it simply disappeared. On either side of the discovery spot its gold content diminished rapidly. But a whole industry was initiated by the kick of that Scotsman's boot.

Within hours after Lamarque had explained McKnight's sudden affluence to the other miners, the hill swarmed with red-shirted men, each frantically digging to see if more of the gold-bearing rock could be found? It was!

Almost everywhere a trench was cut or a shaft sunk on the fifty acres of the hill, more gold-bearing quartz was uncovered. Mostly, as with McKnight's ledge, the pay ore dwindled rapidly away, or, if it did continue to a greater depth, ground water seeping in made further mining impossible. If water did not stop the miner from digging deeper, hard rock did. At a depth of about thirty feet unweathered rock was encountered. Beyond that depth the metavolcanic "country rock" of the area had not been softened by the action of the air, the water, and by the acids of the decaying pine needles. From that depth on, the points of the miners' tools were blunted, and all progress ceased.

But so much gold was taken from the hillside during the first few months of their operations that many of the forty-niners actually thought that it would lose its value as the medium of exchange. For a time the miners went to great lengths to convert their easily gotten gold into silver. They were more familiar with that metal as coinage. They had more faith in its continuing value.

Somewhat over $4,000,000 was sent to the mint, all obtained from the top thirty feet of "Gold Hill" during the two years immediately after McKnight's discovery. Had the wealth continued on into the depths of the earth, as the miners had at first believed, gold might indeed have lost its monetary value.

Between mid-October and Christmas, 1850, the Hugenan brothers dug and pounded out $30,000. They then left the mines temporarily and spent the rest of the winter in Sacramento and in San Francisco, where the action was.

Of course the three brothers had a head start. They had already dug out several tons of the white flat rock to be used for the foundations and the fireplace of the cabin they were building. When they saw the sample of McKnight's treasure rock, they re-examined their building stone more carefully. Sure enough, the yellow specks they had noticed, but had not troubled to investigate, were composed of pure gold. They found other materials for the foundations and for their fireplace.

Grass Valley became the focal point for a new gold rush. Miners by the hundreds left the cold water of the placer mines to look for the gold buried in the white rock.

Much more than Gold Hill soon became involved. A hundred ledges on either side of Wolf Creek were uncovered. The Allison Ranch Mine three miles downstream from the original discovery was eventually followed to a great depth. It produced almost a million ounces of gold before it was finally closed in the early 1900s.

On LaFayette Hill, immediately south of Gold Hill, numerous ledges were located. Eventually, they were all consolidated into the North Star property and worked from the main shaft of that mine.

North and east of the town of Grass Valley a prospector found a great contact ledge. From this vein of broken quartz, the Eureka, the Brunswick, and the Idaho-Maryland Mines combined to produce more than $100,000,000 in bullion before the fixed price of gold and the postwar inflation forced them to cease operations.

But the greatest bonanza of all was the Empire system of quartz ledges. The main shaft of the Empire Mine itself was located just half a mile north and west of the McGuire placer mining claims. The ledge skirted the McGuire property to the west. In places profitable mines operated within a hundred yards of the property lines. Eventually, the chain of mines along the ledge system was taken over by the Empire. The underground workings were connected and all operations were carried on through the Empire's main shaft. The drifts and shafts extended under all of Osborn Hill to the south, and under the entire city of Grass Valley to the north. To the west, drifts eventually were extended until they made contact with those of the North Star Mine system. The McGuire and other privately owned property stopped their operations to the east. The drifts, shafts, and stopes totaled a staggering two hundred or more miles through the hard rock of the Sierra foothills before the closing of the mines. More than $200,000,000 was hoisted from depths as great as ten thousand feet through the Empire shaft alone.

Truth, it is said, is often stranger than fiction. So it is a fact that, although the McGuire property was completely surrounded by some of the world's most productive gold mines, no paying ledges were ever discovered on the McGuire placer claims. They remained surface mining claims until all the gold was scraped off the bedrock. Then the claims were patented as an agricultural homestead under the law pushed through Congress by Mr. Lincoln in 1864.

To the mining fraternity, this was not surprising. All the McGuire property, save the few acres where the creek had cut to bedrock and where the placer gold was found, was covered by a post-Eocene deposit of volcanic ash. This made the exposure of any quartz ledges by surface exploration quite impossible. It was this same ash, however, that had buried the ancient river channel, holding the gold in nature's time vault, only to be unlocked and the gold released to the modern argonauts.

Many other seemingly barren spots existed in the twenty-five square miles that comprised the Grass Valley Lode Mining district. Therefore the McGuire family never thought itself justified in taking the great gamble necessary to explore the property deep underground. In retrospect, it seems probable that others did. With mines operating underground within feet of the property lines it is most likely that at least one of them made the "mistake" of following the ledge on which they were working across the property lines.

One mine, whose shaft was less than a quarter mile to the north, suddenly ceased mining in 1916. Its workings were allowed to fill with water, and the collar of the shaft was dynamited. This made it impossible for an engineer to make a survey to find if indeed the mine had confined its digging to its own property.

It was common knowledge that the mine had struck an extremely large pocket of highgrade ore just before operations were abandoned. This in itself made the mine suspect, but when, at the close of World War I, the family that had owned the mine invested several million dollars in the construction of the newest and most modern of the San Francisco hotels, the suspicions of the people of Grass Valley would seem to have been confirmed. The mine had taken the gold from under the Empire or the McGuire property. The owners had then destroyed the mine to keep the truth from being exposed. By the time the truth leaked out it was, of course, too late for anyone to do anything about it.

In 1938, it was discovered that the Empire was working within a very few feet of the western line of the McGuire property. Using this bit of information, the family had no difficulty selling the mineral rights to the Idaho-Maryland Mine. The property had long been for sale for $100,000. The Idaho-Maryland was not interested in the surface. They paid $75,000 for the minerals. They expected to explore the property, working from the Brunswick shaft, located to the north and east. World War II and inflation intervened. No drifting was ever done and no shafts were ever sunk. The gold, if there ever was any, is still there!

In 1967, the surface, which the Idaho-Maryland would not buy for $25,000, was sold to a land subdivider for $210,000!

McGuire was repeatedly approached by promoters with schemes to increase the size of his placer mining operations and invest the sure profits in the development of rich quartz ledges. He never succumbed to the temptation. He preferred to live the quiet life, mining in the winter until he had recovered enough gold to carry his family through the following year. Then he turned to his farming. This was work he loved. That, and the love he had for his ever-increasing family, made life complete. Who could ask for more?

McGuire was quick to see that mining quartz ledges presented great risks. Few men could resist the temptation of following the vein to greater depth after the first pocket or chimney had been worked out. Each man knew that just one more "round" would bring down more of the gold-studded rock. Often it did! But more often it did not!

A visit to the Greenwood Cemetery in Grass Valley will give proof of the tragic results of such blind hopes. There, in an area enclosed by a cast iron fence, are the graves of Michael and Helen Brannon, and their four children. All of the headstones bear the same date: July 20, 1857.

Brannon arrived in Grass Valley almost simultaneously with McKnight's discovery. He staked a location on LaFayette Hill and almost immediately uncovered an eighteen-inch quartz ledge that quickly gave up several thousand dollars in gold. At a depth of thirty-five feet the value of the ore decreased, and the unaltered rock became too hard to mine without better equipment. Brannon used the money he had accumulated to return to Boston. There he organized a company that was to furnish the money needed to buy the mining machinery. Then he returned to California with his wife and family.

The ledge continued to be barren except for minor pockets. Repeatedly the Boston backers sent more money to keep the mine going. Surely, just a few more feet would bring the drift to a pocket of major importance.

Eventually, the fatal day arrived. A letter came from the East. No more funds would be advanced.

Brannon sold his house and borrowed every cent that he could to keep the mine operating. It was to no avail. He found no more gold. Using the grocery money from his wife's cookie jar, he sent to Sacramento for a bottle of prussic acid. This he mixed with the breakfast gruel he had cooked for the family. He ate none himself, but walked to the working face of his mine and touched off the final charge of blasting powder. Friends found his broken body covered by the shattered quartz brought down by the last blast.

One story of the tragedy states that the quartz that covered the body was heavy with the gold that Brannon had at last decided fate had denied him. Another, and a more likely story, says that at last he had found the elusive pay shoot. He rushed to town to show the banker a sample of the ore to prove that at last he could pay his overdue notes, and asked for "eating money" to tide him over until he could get some of the rich ore to the mill. The banker refused and foreclosed on the loans.

The disappointment was too great. Brannon, in a fit of despondency and frustration, murdered his family, and then committed suicide.

Regardless of which story is believed, it is known that when the North Star Mine consolidated with the Gold Hill and the LaFayette Hill properties, and prospected from the three-thousand-foot level, the Brannon ledge was found. It produced many millions as it was worked upward to near where Brannon had set off the fatal charge. It was also followed down to near the ten-thousand-foot level, producing rich ore to that depth!

The consolidation and successful operation of these properties was carried out by A. B. Foote, the "hero" of *Angle of Repose*, William Stegner's Pulitzer Prize Novel (1970). A. B. Foote was the grandfather of the fictional character who was supposed to have returned to the Foote Mansion (North Star Mansion) to live out his remaining days and to research the writings of his grandmother. She had been a successful writer and illustrator. Stegner used fictitious names. The mine was called the "Zodiac Mine." But the people of Grass Valley know all too well who the real characters were. Many of them were not too pleased with some of the liberties taken with the morals and psychic abnormalities of the first Foote generation!

McGuire did do some digging to see if any of the rich ledges outcropped under the volcanic ash. Mainly, however, he confined his prospecting to endeavoring to find the "lead" to the channel of Eocene gravel, of which the gravel that he did mine was but an isolated bench or bar.

From the beginning he found broken pieces of quartz that showed specks of gold. After McKnight's discovery, he saved and panned these stray specimens. He realized that these had been broken off from ledges on Osborn Hill above and had been carried down onto his property by the flashfloods from the winter storms. When he tried to find the source of these bits of quartz, he was too late. The hill already swarmed with miners who could not find a place to dig on Gold Hill and had spilled over onto other ridges that might expose more quartz ledges. Almost immediately someone uncovered a rich outcropping and within forty-eight hours there was barely standing space on the hill. Shortly the hill was pocketed with trenches and shafts. Naturally, disputes arose over the ownership of the richest ledges. A full-scale civil war was fought over the richest claims (the "Osborn Hill War.") A dozen or more men were killed. One local dentist in protecting his brother's property emptied his six shooter into a group of would-be claim jumpers. Either they were very close or he was an expert with his shooting iron. He killed five men with the six shots. A sixth was seriously wounded. That claim was never molested again!

Once Michael had learned enough about mining, and had learned something of the sources of the gold in the placer mines, he began a serious search for the channel of the ancient river or creek that had carried the smooth, water-worn gold to his diggings.

From the first miners had found gold in gravel high on the canyon walls of the gold-bearing rivers. They needed no geologists to tell them that at some earlier time the river had changed its course before it could undermine and carry away the gravel bars that it always built up on the interior of its bends. As the stream cut deeper, the bar was left progressively higher on the canyon wall. It now became a "bench."

The men mining the benches were responsible for the discovery of the ancient Eocene river gravels. Periodically, they found a bench in which the gravel was compacted, and in some cases cemented so tightly that it had to be crushed in a stamp mill before the gold it carried could be released. In addition, most of these compacted benches when followed did not parallel the canyon walls. Instead they seemed to go straight into the mountainside, disappearing under lava flows or under great thicknesses of other volcanic deposits. Often they carried so much gold that it was profitable to quarry out or to mine the gravel exactly as coal is mined.

By the mid-1850s, students of the new science of geology began to investigate the goldfields. Their studies showed that the quartz pebbles in the compacted gravels was of very ancient origin. Further studies explained the source of the gold in the so-called "Blue Channels."

Some two million years ago the land form now occupied by the Sierra Nevada Mountains was relatively flat. It was traversed by streams running from east to west, roughly paralleling the present small rivers tributary to the Sacramento and the San Joaquin rivers. At what is now the 3,000-foot elevation in the north, in the region off the Feather River, and at 1,500-feet south along the Fresno River, the "Eocene rivers" broke out of the steeper country to the east, where they had for millions of years been eroding the hills away and mining the great gold-bearing quartz ledges, which must have made up a large percentage of the mountain ranges. When the rush of the water was checked by a lessening of the grade, the heavy gold was deposited.

The gradual change in the elevations at which the Eocene gravel was found at first fooled the scientiests. They surmised that one great river, one probably ten times as large as the present Columbia, flowed from north to south through the gently sloping land of what is now the Sierra foothills. The great river, they thought, came from somewhere in Canada. All traces of its existence north of the Feather River had been buried by the great volcanic eruptions that formed the plateau regions of Washington and of Oregon. Some geologists even hypothecated that the super river eventually turned and flowed north through the San Joaquin valley and out through the Golden Gate into the Pacific. They believed that the present Columbia is the remnant of the Eocene river. Eventually it was dammed by a lava flow and forced to the west at Walla Walla, Washington. It found a passage through the Cascades north of Mount Hood and on to the ocean.

McGuire subscribed to the Columbian theory. Therefore if he could but find the channel that had carried the gold to his claims, he could follow it north under the thick ash deposit that made up Cedar Ridge and Union Hill. There it would provide him with an inexhaustible supply of rich gravel. But he and his sons were doomed to disappointment. What he really was mining was a very small bench left by the forerunner of the present Yuba River.

Mike, Michael's youngest son, never did give up completely in his effort to locate the elusive channel. As late as 1949, the writer helped him sink a shaft near the junction of Colfax Highway (State Route 127) and Rattlesnake Road, in a vain search for the nonexistent channel. The writer's time was not wasted. In 1968, he subdivided a part of the McGuire Ranch into acre lots. Because of his mining experience on the property he was able to guarantee the buyers that they could get good drinking water from wells of less than thirty feet in depth. In fact water was struck at twenty feet in every well drilled in the seemingly solid rock, which was in fact compacted volcanic ash, or in some cases highly fractured metavolcanic rock and diorite.

7

The Catholics

After McKnight's discovery, not much of the quartz was broken into a sand with a hammer. Better methods were quickly found. First, someone broke the ore into half-inch pieces with the hammer, then smashed it to a powder by placing it in an iron kettle and pulverizing it with blunted end of a pick. This quickly gave way to a heavy wooden stick shod with an iron cap.

The Hugenan brothers had so much ore to grind that they had to have a better process. Near Nevada City, they found a large granite rock in which the Indians had formed a mortar for the grinding of their seeds. A teamster hauled the rock over the hill at Town Talk to the edge of Wolf Creek. The pestle was at first a fifty-pound fir pole capped with iron. They soon tired of lifting the pole so that it would fall on the ore in the mortar; so they moved to a place on the creek where there was an overhanging oak limb. Using a rope they tied the pole to the limb and pounded it down by throwing their weight on the pole. When the weight was released, the limb sprang back to its original position, pulling the pole with it. This was much easier on the back, and it was just as efficient. But still it was very slow and laborious. So they put the power of running water to work.

An undershot waterwheel was constructed on the creek. To one end of the axle of the wheel, they fixed an eccentric, which was activated by each turn of the wheel. Around the upper part of the pine pole they fitted a collar, which rode the eccentric up and then was dropped as the high part of the eccentric passed beneath.

Thus was born the first stamp mill. Eventually, stamps were

built in groups of five. This grouping formed a "battery," with all the stamps falling in a common mortar box on a common anvil. Later several batteries were operated in unison, forming a "mill."

Steam engines, and later electric motors, replaced the water-wheels as soon as they became available. The exception to this was the Pelton Waterwheel, several of which continued to be operated in some of the largest mills right up to the closing of the mines in 1957.

The Mexican miners near Sonora and at Mariposa introduced the *arrastre*, or Mexican Mill, to grind their ore. This consisted of a circular trough of smooth stones. A mule dragged a large heavy rock around and around the circle, crushing the ore that had been placed in the trough. The stamp mill proved to be much more efficient. The *arrastre* was never used to any great extent in the northern mines.

During the period between 1919 and 1948, the Empire Mine operated a mill consisting of 80 stamps, each weighing 1,800 pounds. They had a drop of 16 inches, and each stamp fell at the rate of 45 times per minute. The mill ran continuously, 24 hours each day and 365 days a year. Only one battery at a time was closed down to make repairs and to clean the accumulated gold and amalgam from the battery box, and from the amalgamation table below the stamps.

The roar of the falling stamps was clearly heard in the town of Grass Valley two miles to the north. The people of the community became so accustomed to the distant rumble that they failed to notice it. Only if for some reason the mill was forced to stop the falling of the stamps, did they realize that the noise had existed in the first place.

At 1:30 A.M. on Christmas morning, 1935, an accident at the mill forced the cutting off of all the electric power. Everyone in the town of five thousand knew immediately that something was wrong at the Empire. Those who had retired and were already asleep were startled into wakefulness by the sudden silence!

It seems that one of the mill men had a few too many Tom and Jerrys before going on shift at midnight. When the ore in one of the bins failed to feed down properly, he climbed into the container below the one thousand tons of broken ore and proceeded to break it loose with a steel bar. Had he had his normal reactions he would have been able to climb clear of the sliding mass of ore in plenty of time. Alcohol, however, had interfered. He missed the first step on the ladder and, before he could recover, he had been pinned against the lower wall of the bin.

When he was missed, the foreman searched for him and eventually discovered one hand sticking out above the crushed quartz. He immediately pulled the master switch to liberate every available man in a fruitless effort to dig out the victim of the strange and needless accident.

Eventually, the stamp mill became obsolete. Cone crushers, combined with rod and ball mills, were substituted for the stamps. These, combined with the flotation cells, proved to be much more efficient for the grinding of the ore and for the recovery of the values from the pulverized material. The stamps, the amalgamation tables, and the vibrating Wilfley tables, which had been the ultimate in gold recovery machinery for nearly a hundred years, had to give way to more modern technology.

Meanwhile, McGuire resisted the temptation of trying to become rich by gambling in the mining of the rich quartz ledges that were being found all around his property.

In 1852, he increased the efficiency of his mining operations by installing a "Long Tom." Thereafter he could wash as much as ten yards of gravel per day. Now he could work material that would pay as little as fifty cents per yard. He could also afford to hire help, because wages had fallen to $2 to $3 per day.

The Long Tom was a device similar to the sluice box, the latter being but a long box or trough with cleats nailed across its bottom. The box was set at an angle and a stream of water run through it. Gravel was shoveled in at the upper end. The rushing water carried the mud, rock, and sand through the box. The gold, if any, remained back of the cleats. It is obvious that the successful operation of the sluice box depended on the amount of water available, and on the size of the largest stones in the gravel to be washed. McGuire had only a very small stream to work with, so a sluice box was never practical on his claim.

He could, however, use a Long Tom. It, in effect, consisted of two small sluice boxes, one suspended above the other. The upper and the smaller of the two boxes were fitted with a screened or perforated bottom. Water was piped into the upper box, and gravel shoveled in. The miner stirred the gravel to allow the water and the fine material to pass through the screen into the larger box below. Periodically, he threw out the larger stones and other material that would not pass through the screen, using an ordinary stable fork. With only a small percentage of the material passing through the screen, a much smaller head of water could be used with efficiency.

To increase the amount of gold trapped back of the cleats, mercury was placed in the lower box. It remained on the upper side of the cleats. The water and the sand, being lighter than the mercury, floated across the top of the liquid metal, while the heavier gold sank and was trapped and amalgamated. From time to time the trapped material was scraped out of the box and panned. The mercury and the amalgam were distilled. The mercury came off as a vapor. The gold remained in the retort.

The gold pan, the rocker, the Long Tom, and the sluice box are still standard equipment for placer gold prospecting and mining the world over. Any handyman can make any of the items on location except the pan. It is light enough to be carried. Besides, it makes an excellent wash basin for camping.

Large deposits of gravel are, of course, worked by hydraulic mining, or by dredging. In either case, the gravel is washed into a series of sluice boxes. On the dredgers the sluice boxes become highly sophisticated. Their angle may be increased or decreased to adjust for the nature of the material being mined, and they are vibrated to make for even more efficiency. The principle of separation by washing the gravel and allowing the gold to be trapped has not changed since Jason sought the "Golden Fleece." (In reality, the "Fleece" was only a sheepskin suspended in the rushing current of rivers in Asia Minor. Very fine gold was carried in suspension. In contact with the kinky wool of the fleece, the metal was trapped. It was recovered by rinsing the sheepskin in a container of clear water.)

The first miners in California knew nothing of the principles used for centuries by miners in other gold-producing countries. By necessity they were forced to reinvent mining techniques. They did, however, eventually make many important improvements in the Old World methods, and they were quick to make full use of modern science and technology.

Michael lived until 1906. Until the last two years of his life he managed to recover a little gold each winter. The family no longer depended on him. The farm supplied most of his and Mary's wants. Only during the last few years of his life did he stop searching for the Eocene channel. Even then he directed the boys as they carried on the work during slack periods of employment. He left Mary a small amount of gold, which he had "squirreled" away, and the ranch. She continued to live there until 1910. Then she moved to town to live with her daughter Minnie, and to be near the other children who had remained in the gold-mining town.

Mary lived until 1918. She had lived a long, full life. She had borne ten children, all of whom lived to adulthood, a minor miracle at that time and in that place. Her interest outside of the home and family was centered in the Church.

From the first in California she had not been able to feel comfortable with the miners' wives. They seemed to be from a different world. Mostly they were Protestants, and as such were damned in the hereafter! They, in turn, did not understand her "uppity" ways. Over the years she had refused to shop in the stores of Grass Valley unless Michael had given her a minimum of $100 to spend as she pleased. Most of the miners' wives would have considered themselves fortunate if they were given that much in their entire married lives. Mostly she made her own clothing, but the materials were the best available. Often the local merchants were forced to send to San Francisco to get the yardage goods she had ordered.

"Anyway," the local miners wives reasoned, "if she was so smart, how come she could believe in the infallibility of the Pope? And how could she confess her sins to a strange man in a carefully screened booth? But worst of all, how could she worship the 'idols' which they had been told still occupied positions of importance in the Church. Why, she even prayed to them!" The ignorant Italian and Spanish women, they could understand. They had no way of knowing of anything different. But an educated, intelligent woman like Mary McGuire?

The Catholics of Latin origin did not mix in the Church with the Irish. Even the Bourns, who owned and operated the Empire Mine, were "shanty Irish." Mary had nothing in common with them either. When the second generation of the Bourns took over and built the Irish manor house in the midst of the formal gardens, complete with waterfalls and with reflecting pools, she had grown too old to be of interest to the "new people" who had so suddenly become the leaders of society in Northern California.

She did not live to see Billie Bourn spend a part of his millions in the purchase of the Lakes of Killarney in Ireland, and make a park of the 1,200 acres that surrounded the legendary Lakes. Nor could she know that the "natives," who were most bitter about the rich Yankee taking over their Lakes, would be forced to admit that they had been wrong when Bourn's will was read. It left the Lake Property to his daughter, in trust, during her lifetime. Then it was to revert to the Irish State as a national park!

Mary's one attempt to become friendly with a Grass Valley resident was in 1857. When Lola Montez built her home on Mill Street, Mary heard that she was being snubbed by the local women as an undesirable actress and exotic dancer. She thought this wrong, so she created somewhat of a social scandal when she paid an afternoon call on the former mistress of the king of Bavaria. Later, she did admit that she was curious to see if the story of Lola keeping a bear chained in her garden was true. The bear she was supposed to threaten to turn loose when the women-starved men of the mines became too ardent in their advances. History does not record if she was ever forced to carry out her threat.

Michael heard of the visit and ordered her not to go again. She might have disregarded his instructions, but Father Dalton sent word that he wished to see her. When he told her that it was not fitting for a good Catholic woman to associate with such a notorious character, she obeyed without question. Such was her training.

To understand why Mary, and later the other McGuires, were not among the leaders of the mining community, and why Mary, in particular, did not become part of "Society," it is necessary to know something of the people who did make up a large proportion of the local population.

The Irish Catholics were in a decided minority. True, the Catholic churches in all the early mining towns were well attended, but most of the membership consisted of nationalities almost as foreign to the McGuires as were the "Cousin Jacks," who for most of the years the mines were in operation actually ran the towns. They were Methodists of the most anti-Catholic variety. In addition, they had come from Cornwall, on the south coast of England. That fact alone was enough to prejudice them in the eyes of any self-respecting Irishman.

General Frémont was responsible for the influx of the Cornish miners into the California goldfields. At almost the same time that McKnight had made his discovery on Gold Hill, Frémont found gold in quartz on his ranch near Mariposa. The rock surrounding the quartz in the southern mines was much too hard to work even near the surface, so Frémont went to London immediately to get the tools he knew he must have. While there, someone suggested that since there was no one in California who would know how to use the new equipment, he should try to get a few of the Cornish tin miners to follow him to America and work for him. This he succeeded in doing.

Unfortunately, the Mariposa mines did not go to any depth.

The Cornish miners soon found themselves out of employment. News of the Grass Valley mines had filtered south; so the skilled workmen migrated north to find work.

They were welcomed with open arms by the mine owners who saw gold protruding from the quartz ledges, but who had not the slightest idea of how to go about getting it out of the ground after they had reached a depth where hard unaltered rock was encountered.

The tin miners had worked in much harder rock in the mines of southern England since the time of the Phoenicians. Hard rock mining was the one thing they could do. Naturally they were in great demand. When a good worker was asked if he knew where other good miners could be found, his reply always was, "Well, me 'cousin Jack' back in Cornwall wouldst come, should ye guarantee 'is passage, and gives' im a full year's work."

All Cornish miners thereafter became "Cousin Jacks." Their descendants are so called to this day. When their wives later joined them in the New World, they could be nothing other than "Cousin Jennies."

For many years after the mines became industrialized, the Cousin Jacks held an almost complete monopoly on the jobs. Fathers taught their sons and their nephews. No others knew the trade. When openings occurred in the mines, the "union" allowed no one other than a Cornishman to go to work.

The management knew that costly accidents happened when someone not approved by the foreman, who was always a Cousin Jack, was put to work. In effect, Grass Valley, became a "company town" in reverse. Only approved persons could work there, but the workers decided who that should be, not the management.

To demonstrate how completely the Cousin Jacks controlled the situation, one needs only to recall that in the late 1920s, when there was a revival of the anti-Catholic branch of the Ku Klux Klan, crosses were frequently burned on the hillsides of western Nevada County.

The Cousin Jacks and the Cousin Jennies also controlled the

two semihistorical societies known as the Native Sons and the Native Daughters of the Golden West. Having complete control, they were able to "unwrite" and distort history!

In 1929, the societies had a plaque cast and placed on a stone monument erected on Gold Hill to commemorate the discovery of gold on that spot in 1850 by George McKnight. But damned if the men and the women in charge of having the plaque cast were about to let anyone but a true son of Cornwall get the credit for the history-making discovery. (Besides they mistakenly thought that the "Mc" indicated that he was Irish. Ergo, he was a Catholic.) They had the "Mc" left out of the name. The plaque reads " 'George Knight' discovered Gold near This Spot in 1850."

The length to which the bigotry was carried is illustrated by the fact that when Marian McGuire, Michael Junior's daughter, graduated from the University of California in 1929, and applied for a teaching position in the Grass Valley High School, she was not considered for the position because she was Catholic, and members of that faith were not allowed to teach in the local schools if there was any way to prevent it. Rumor has it that Mike changed some minds when he let it be known that if she did not get the position, he would publish some of the things he knew as to how some members of the school board had acquired the wealth that allowed them to live in comfort, or the money they had used to start their current businesses. He knew, because he had worked at the Empire Mine during the time when each had "highgraded" his wealth from the Empire Mill!

The board suddenly decided that, since she was a Catholic, she would know better the Latin, which she would be teaching, than would any of the other applicants who had not had the advantage of being exposed to that language several times each week.

Two years later, however, when it became known that she was about to marry a non-Catholic teacher in the same school, he was fired. He was considered an undesirable influence on the youth of the community. He might not embrace Catholicism, but he most certainly did not understand the philosophy of that

Church. Therefore he must not be very intelligent and not a suitable teacher for their sons and daughters.

Mary McGuire's death was in part due to the great influenza epidemic of 1918. Some of her children had been a great disappointment to her. On the other hand, four of her offspring had made her most proud.

Jim had become famous throughout the world as a mining engineer, and an advisor to the President. Minnie had gained recognition as a teacher of teachers. Tom had become a civil engineer well known in Northern California. Unfortunately Mary did not live to see Michael Junior make an important contribution to the mining industry of California and of the world.

Part 2

The Progeny

1

Joseph (the Prospector)

Joe, the oldest of the McGuire brood, did not go beyond the sixth grade at the Union Hill School. He was a big strong boy. At that time when a boy was big enough and strong enough to go to work he was old enough. Age was never a factor in hiring; just the ability to do the work.

He, like the nine who were to follow, survived the usual childhood diseases as well as the real hazards of growing up in the wild new country where disaster could, and often did strike from every side. Loaded guns left unattended were common, and gun play resulting in murder often did take place on Osborn Hill, which in reality was the play yard of the McGuire children. Blasting powder was stored in a hundred places within a mile of the McGuire home, and other hazards inherent to a mining country were omnipresent.*

---

*In 1922, Mike lost a small dog while cutting wood on the lower slopes of Osborn Hill. Three days later, Marian and Jim, his children, were led to an abandoned mine shaft by the sound of very faint barking. There, at a depth of twenty-five feet, alive and unhurt, but very hungry, was the lost family pet. Fortunately, it was in the late fall. Otherwise the shaft would have been a well and the dog would have drowned. Although the law made it mandatory for all such shafts to be filled, or at least carefully fenced, many cave-ins occurred, and many fences are still not kept in good repair. Numerous open shafts are still to be found on or near the McGuire property where the children played. As recently as 1970, a survey party almost fell into a shaft that years ago had been converted to a well by placing masonry around its collar. Its location had been unknown for a hundred years, although it was within fifteen feet of the well-traveled Osborn Hill Road. The opening was so well covered by brush that it was and had been completely hidden for a century.

As were all the McGuires who were to follow, Joe was a fighter. It was well that this was so, for the Irish were in the minority even in the Union Hill District, and a trip into town was an adventure not to be undertaken lightly by a child, unless accompanied by parents, or unless, as was usually the case, a gang made the foray.

Mostly the parents stood aloof from the squabbles. Only when the bullies began to get too rough with some of the smaller children did they intercede. The philosophy was: "Life at best, is a struggle. This fact every schoolboy should recognize. He must learn to protect himself, and to help protect the weak, if they were related; otherwise it was usually best not to interfere. A few black eyes and bloody noses were but a part of growing up."

The young McGuires were forced to protect themselves endlessly simply because they were Irish at a time when the great potato famine in Ireland had loaded every ship with the poor, desperate, starving people. Mostly they came to the New World. They landed in New York or in Boston penniless and hungry. The shrewd Yankees took advantage of their desperate straits and employed them at a wage that made living under any but the most depraved conditions impossible. Mostly they congregated in makeshift shelters along the railroad right of ways, where they were employed as track maintenance workers. Hence they became the "shanty Irish," subject to the ridicule of everyone who was fortunate enough to occupy a more advantageous position. An Irish family might well live in the best house in town, but once off their own property they were automatically classified with their unfortunate countrymen, the latest of the long line of uneducated, uncouth laborers imported to do the menial work of the growing nation.

The McGuire boys were also Catholic. This in turn made them alien. Mostly the children in the neighborhood were Cousin Jacks; therefore they hated the Irish Catholics. Those whose parents had not come from Cornwall were from areas influenced by the New England Puritans, or by the Midwestern and Southern people, from what later came to be known as the "Bible Belt."

From the first, Michael and Mary had instilled a sense of pride in the heritage of their children. They told them very little about their ancestors in Ireland, but they did assure them that they came from a long line of "Fighting Irish," and that was something they should never forget!*

The religious training of the children was left to the Church, except that Mary saw to it that the habit of attending Mass each Sunday was firmly established; come "hell or high water" somehow every member of the family went to church. This habit they practiced throughout their entire lives. They also saw to it that their own children were indoctrinated in the same manner.

At the beginning of the Gold Rush, the Church was quick to see that there would be a need for priests in the new country, and it was ready and able to grasp the opportunity to be on the spot when its services were needed. At one time it was a common jest in the gold country to "watch where a new Catholic church was being built. Stake a claim there at once, as there was sure to be rich diggings close by!"

Of course, the Church did not have an inside source of information as to the location of the gold, but it did have an excellent "spy" system. The "spies" funneled the information about new strikes straight to the authorities, which were empowered to be the first on location to gain the goodwill of the miners who had money to "throw away." The reasoning was: "the Church should be there to catch part of the windfall!"

The potato famine had made for a great excess of priests in Ireland. The Church took advantage of the situation to relieve the oversupply there, and to staff the new churches in California,

---

*A great-granddaughter, Maridale Calhoon, in Ireland very briefly in 1955, attempted to delve into the family history. She found no record of the marriage of Michael McGuire and Mary Cavanaugh in the year 1847, or thereabouts, in County Cork. The only clue she had to work from was the fact that Mary, when she became angry at Michael, accused him of being a "stubborn old Corkorian."

there to build churches and to minister to the spiritual needs of the people, especially the Irish and those of Latin origin.

That the Mother Church chose well in sending the Irish priests is proven by the fact that, almost without exception, the first and the most pretentious of the churches built were Catholic. And the last to be abandoned, when the "camps" became ghost towns, were also those with ties to Rome.

A large part of the Fathers' success was, of course, due to the fact that their "underground" sources of information told them of every miner's success. If the lucky miner was a Protestant, the priest appeared with hat in hand, asking for aid for the poor of the community. The priest naturally was the poorest of the poor, and he had no qualms when he diverted a portion of the "widow and orphans funds" for the living expenses of the clergy. If the miner was a Catholic the priest made no request; he simply told the lucky man how much he was expected to contribute to whatever Church project was being carried out at that time.

This practice of the Irish priests was one of the main reasons why Michael McGuire never succumbed to the temptation of mining his claim on a large scale. Not only was the gold safe under the five to ten feet of topsoil where no thief could ever reach it; it was out of the reach of the grasping Churchmen as well! He did contribute on a regular basis to whatever the special need of the Church was at the moment, as well as to the everyday operations of the parish. When the Saint Mary's convent and school was built in the late 1860s, he worked a few extra days on his claim and turned all the gold recovered over to the Sisters.

Mary was disappointed when Joe refused to go beyond the sixth grade, the highest being taught at the Union Hill school. She tried to influence him to continue, but to no avail. He insisted that his father needed the help, but mainly he was eager to learn all there was to know about mining. He was already looking forward to the time when he could go into the mountains to look for a mine of his own.

Because of the closeness of the properties, the Empire Mine had always tried to maintain a friendly relationship with the

McGuires. At sixteen, Joe, although he was not a Cousin Jack, was allowed to go to work underground in that mine. There he learned to swing the "single jack," a five-pound hammer held in one hand to strike a steel drill, held by and turned by the other hand. Later he was trained in the use of the "Double Jack," a sixteen-pound sledgehammer, swung with both hands to strike, in rhythm with another miner, a larger steel drill held and turned by a third man.

This was hard, back-breaking work. As soon as possible Joe became a powder man. He learned to place the blasting powder in the drill holes, and to cut the fuses into lengths sufficient to have them fire in the proper sequences to give the maximum breaking effect.

Finally, after gaining additional experience as a "timber man," shoring up the "weak ground" where rocks might fall and crush a miner, he knew that he had learned all that he could in Grass Valley. He quit the Empire and applied for a job as a foreman in a silver mine in Virginia City, Nevada.

He was employed immediately. He was among the forerunners of a long line of mining men, including the future President, Herbert Hoover, who worked in the mines in Nevada County to gain practical experience, then went on to improve the mining techniques of mines the world over.

Any man with proof of practical experience in the progressive mines of Nevada County was welcomed anywhere that underground work was being done. If he proved to be a sober workman, he was almost always promoted to a foreman within a short time. More often he was hired as such in the first place.

Between 1876 and 1898, Joe alternated between working in the Virginia City silver mines, the copper and gold mines of Montana, and in Idaho's lead mines. His was a restless soul. Periodically, he saved a stake and took to the hills prospecting.

In 1889, he joined the rush to Alaska. Once he reached Cripple Creek, his services were in great demand. He knew how to recover the gold the sourdoughs had discovered. Ninety-nine percent of the men who had gone north had never seen "gold

in the raw." They had not the slightest idea of how to recover
the values their pans showed them to be in their claims.

The owner of a rich gravel bar who had the good fortune to
meet McGuire when he arrived on the scene was also smart
enough to hire him on the spot at a wage he could not refuse.
The owner also had the good sense to overlook the extra large
nugget that Joe slipped into his own pocket from time to time.
He had heard that this was a sanctioned practice in California.
Joe did not look on the practice as stealing.

In addition the mine owner found that the best way to ensure
his foreman's continued services was to foot his bar bills when
he took off to do a little hell raising with Klondike Kate and
with the other girls in the Dawson saloons. As a result, Joe was
always too drunk, or too sick from the last escapade, to think of
going off to look for a mine of his own.

At the end of two and a half years, Joe found that the sunny
climes of California held much more appeal than did the gold
of Alaska, even when combined with the free liquor and with
the women of easy virtue. In addition he had enough of those
extra nuggets to supply his simple wants. He took the first steamer
down the Yukon in the spring of 1902. Eventually he made his
way back to Grass Valley.

Joe's nuggets did not last long. He attempted to start a prohibition movement of his own by drinking up all the available
liquor in the towns he visited. He did not succeed. Shortly he
was forced to return to work.

Tonopah, Nevada, was the gold rush center at that time.
There he worked for a short time underground. Mostly he roamed
the desert and the mountains of central Nevada looking for more
paying ledges.

He found some too! But he was not interested in working
them for the gold they contained. He had passed the stage where
he had had visions of working a mine and becoming a millionaire.
His perpetual thirst demanded that immediate cash be realized.
Anyway, he had inherited some of the Irish luck. He could always
find another mine. Perhaps the next one he would settle down

and work. He never did. He continued to sell each prospect to the highest bidder. Then, just as immediately he went on a hell-raising, bar-busting, drunk.*

At the beginning of World War I, Joe returned to Grass Valley to take a surface job at the Empire Mine, the same mine where the neighborhood boy had learned to mine years before. The manpower shortage had forced the mine to hire almost anyone, in its attempt to keep open and operating.

In mid-1918, Joe was killed in a gunfight. Rumor had it that a miner who was supposed to be working deep underground, and therefore safely out of the way, had returned home unexpectedly. Joe did not get away from his amorous pursuits quickly enough. He had spent too much time fighting the bottle to be able to hold his own with the irate husband. The fight was made even more uneven by the fact that the miner was armed with a forty-five!

For the record, Joe was killed accidentally in a drunken argument following a poker game.

The family always thought that Joe's wildness and his tragic death contributed to Mary's passing. She had been living in her memories for several years. Tim, her second son, had already been killed under strange circumstances. Now her firstborn had disgraced the family name. The fact that some of the others had been a credit to the McGuire name did not lessen her grief. The medical report said that she died from complications following the flu. But the family knew better. She died of a broken heart.

---

*When Marian Calhoon, Mike Junior's daughter, visited Tonopah in 1963, she found several old-timers basking in the bright desert sun in front of the Pioneer Saloon. Yes, they remembered a wild Irishman by the name of McGuire, who came to town after selling each of his newly discovered claims. He drank and whored until his money ran out, or until he was arrested for the destruction of property and fined to the extent of all his remaining funds, in which case the judge always loaned him enough money to grub-stake his next expedition into the desert.

2

Tim (The Hydraulic Miner)

Michael had been correct when he had surmised that Mary would lose her girlish figure shortly after they arrived in California. Early in 1851, a miner's wife from Boston Ravine, acting as midwife, delivered another fine baby boy.

This one they named Tim (Timothy). He was a carbon copy of his older brother. He also survived the hazards of growing up in the rough mining country and, like Joe, went to work, first helping his father mine and farm, then drawing a man's wage in the mines as soon as he was large enough. He deviated from Joe in only one respect: He did not go underground. The easy-to-get placer gold was of much more interest to him than the elusive veins of quartz, which might, and again might not, carry gold.

At sixteen he went to work for the Michigan Bluff Mining Company at their hydraulic mine, on Greenhorn Creek, near the little town of Red Dog. He lived in a boardinghouse in the town, which boasted a population of five-thousand. It also had a very bad reputation, even in the wild mining country, because it claimed the usual assortment of blacksmith shops and stores and sixteen saloons, but no churches! The saloons were the only two-story buildings in the town. The upper floors were reserved for the saloon girls—girls who would have been grossly insulted if they had been asked to serve drinks to the patrons of the establishments, like the saloon girls now pictured on television.

The town's second claim to fame was the fact that, in 1876, the entire town was moved, building by building, to the site of its neighbor and competitor, "You bet," a mile and a half away.

This was to allow the rich gravel that covered the bedrock under the buildings to be mined. The buildings were never returned.

Because there was no church in Red Dog, Tim was required to walk the ten miles over the hills to Grass Valley each Sunday to attend Mass with the family. Mary insisted on that. When Mary issued an edict, Mary was obeyed!

At the mine, Tim at first helped the tunnel men drive a drift back under the cliffs of Eocene gravel, which at this location had been laid down in deposits more than two hundred feet thick. The geologists explain that great deposit by saying that, during the time the river was carrying its gold-bearing gravel, a volcanic eruption had poured out a long tongue of lava that flowed across the river valley. When the lava cooled, a dam several hundred feet in height was formed. There the rushing water of the river was checked by the still water of the lake that had been formed. With the slowing of the current, its load was dropped, forming the great deposits of stratified gravel and sand on the lake bottom.

A million or so years later, another eruption, or series of eruptions, exploded hundreds of cubic miles of volcanic ash high into the air. As the material fell back to earth, it filled both the lake and the channel of the rivers leading into it, as well as the valley downstream below the lava dam. Subsequent eruptions showered down additional volcanic debris, burying the entire countryside under hundreds of feet of ash, exactly as the city of Pompeii was entombed by the eruption of Vesuvius in 28 A.D.

At the end of the tunnels that Tim helped to dig, the miners placed tons of blasting powder. The tunnels were then refilled and the powder exploded. Often as much as a million tons of the overlying gravel was shaken loose, to be more easily washed away by the water blasting out of the throats of the hydraulic monitors.

The volcanic overburden was allowed to flow directly into the stream below the mine. The gravel was directed through sluice boxes. These were often four feet wide and four feet deep. They extended for miles below the mine in an attempt to recover all the gold possible before the gravel was allowed to escape into the stream channels. Eventually, the gravel, like the overburden materials, was deposited in the Sacramento Valley, where it choked the rivers and covered good ranchland to a depth of thirty feet or more.

Tim had been fascinated by the workings of the hydraulic mines from the first time he saw the rush of water from the monitor doing a hundred times as much work as he and his father could do by the hardest kind of labor. At every opportunity he had walked all the way to the slopes north of Deer Creek at Nevada City to watch the first of the attempts to make the force of running water move the gravel into and through the sluice boxes. Later he was able to see the same methods applied to the slopes just below the great contact ledge being mined by the Eureka Company.

He never tired of listening to the men argue as to just who should be credited with putting the first hydraulic mine into operation, Chabot at Nevada City, or Haskins at Grass Valley. The truth, he decided, was that they should probably receive equal honors: Chabot for being the first to use a canvas hose to direct the water to the point desired, and Haskins for seeing the need for greater pressures and taking the stove pipe from his cabin to make the first metal pipe for the delivery of the water. Some even suggested that Matteson should be recognized, because he was the first to bring water to his mine in a wooden flume and developed some pressure by covering the last few feet of his flume, thus making it a square wooden tube.

In any case, Joe's interest in that type of mining, and his quick grasp of the fundamentals involved, led to his early promotion to the "swing bar" of one of the giant monitors. Here, much more than holding the nozzle steady was involved. The amount of gravel that could be washed during a day could be greatly increased by the judicious directing of the stream of water to exactly the right spots to allow it to undercut and carry away the banks of gravel.

Tim worked with a purpose in mind. He would learn all there was to know about the operation of a hydraulic mine. Then he would find a gravel deposit and start a mine of his own. At the age of nineteen he quit the mine and started prospecting the broken country along the canyon walls of the Yuba and the Feather rivers.

The Irish luck held! Within a year he located a bench of Eocene gravel high on the canyon walls of the Middle Yuba River. His find was located midway between Washington and Downieville, the booming mining towns on the rivers where gold from the ancient channels had been concentrated. He had followed a string of colors up the canyon wall above a particularly rich diggings on the river. At about a hundred feet below the crest, bits of gold stopped appearing in his pan. Just below that point he dug into the bank and found a deposit of Eocene gravel. It carried enough gold to make it worthwhile to mine, but he was not interested in digging out just a few dollars a day. He must see if his find was indeed a buried channel, or an isolated bench, as was the McGuire mine on Little Wolf Creek.

He worked feverishly as he dug a tunnel into the hillside. His luck still held. The gravel did continue into the bank below the covering of compacted volcanic ash. At the end of the tunnel he dug to either side and found that the channel was about a hundred feet wide at this point—certainly large enough to justify the cost of bringing water in from the mountains above to mine by the hydraulic method.

To develop the mine he would need much more money than he or his family and his friends could raise. He must form a mining company.

For a full year he dug gravel and, with the aid of three pack mules, carried it down to a creek below, where he ran it through a Long Tom and panned the concentrates from back of the riffles. He recovered about $1.50 per yard from the ordinary gravel. The scrapings from the bedrock carried much more. Occasionally it produced a nugget large enough to be saved for selling "bait" when the company was organized.

At the end of the year of back-breaking labor, Tim had the money needed for promotion and for expenses. He blocked the mouth of the tunnel and set out on a money-raising expedition. On the way out of the mining country he stopped at Nevada City to make sure that his claim had been properly recorded and to file claims on additional nearby land. Then he took the stage to Colfax and rode the Central Pacific train to San Francisco.

On Montgomery Street, Tim had no trouble raising all the money he would need to dig a ditch to the river ten miles above his mine for the delivery of water under two hundred feet of hydrostatic head. Additional money was also needed to buy the pipe, the lumber, and all the hundred other items needed to start the water blasting at the gravel bank.

Tim had never been in Ireland, but he had "kissed the Blarney Stone" by proxy. His glib tongue held the willing listeners, and the size of his nuggets hypnotized them into forcing their money into his bank account. The times were such that intelligent men were taking seemingly foolhardy chances in investing their money. But if the risks were great, the returns were often greater. Of one thing the investor could be sure: the money invested would be used to develop the mine. The era of the "suede shoe" operator had not as yet arrived. True, some outright frauds had been perpetrated, but too often the would-be swindler had been caught and dangled from the limb of the nearest oak tree. Not many men were tempted by that method of getting rich quick.

Back in Marysville, Tim hired the wagons and the teams needed to haul the equipment to the mine. He also engaged the men who would stay in the mountains and put the mine into operation.

Tim had left the mountains in November before the heavy snow of the winter. On May 1 of the following year, his little caravan commenced its trip up the "Great Highway," the toll road that had been cut along the ridge between the North and Middle Forks of the Yuba River. It crossed the Sierra crest at Hennesse Pass, and continued on to the silver mines at Virginia City in Nevada.

Ten miles above his mine, Tim left the main road and cut a new road down to his claims. When the wagons arrived at the site he had selected for the mine buildings, he found that his Irish luck had at last deserted him.

The area was occupied by a well-known gang of cutthroats who operated out of Nigger Tent, the reported headquarters of the nefarious Mrs. Romagi, an ex-madam. She masterminded the operations of the robber gangs that levied an additional toll on the wagon trains hauling supplies to the Nevada mines.

Tim was met by the leader of the gang. He was given a choice. He could fight and take a bullet through his head within five minutes. He could withdraw peacefully and fight his case in the courts in Nevada City, in which case he could expect to get a bullet in his back if it began to look as if he was about to win his case; or he could accept the inevitable. He could sell his supplies to the bandits at a reasonable price and go look for another mine!

Tim made a quick appraisal of the situation and decided not to press his luck. He was sure that he would have no trouble finding another "lead," and the offer made by the bandits for his wagonloads of supplies would be sufficient to pay off the San Francisco investors and give him a grubstake for the search for the new mine. He decided to take his father's advice: "Sometimes running is the only practical solution. It's almost always better to be a live coward than a dead hero!"

He accepted the offer. He took the offered gold, gold that he knew had come from his own mine, and gave the robbers a deed to the mining property along with a bill of sale for the supplies. In effect, he traded his life for the papers that would make the outlaws respectable businessmen.

He paid the miners and the teamsters he had hired and sent them back to Marysville. Next he visited the Wells Fargo office in Nevada City and transferred enough gold to San Francisco to pay off his backers. Finally, he bought a new prospecting outfit at the Alpha Hardware Company. Then after a good drunk to celebrate being alive, he struck out for the hills once more.

He worked up and down the walls of the canyons of the Yuba and Feather rivers for three more years. He got nothing. The stake, which he had been so sure would last until he could find another rich lead, was gone, and he was down to begging grubstakes from the local storekeepers.

Meanwhile, "back at the mine," the bandits had made it big. There is no record of the amount of gold they did take out, but it was enough to allow them to turn respectable, some to go into business in the mining towns, and others to buy large acreages in the foothill country and become "landed gentry."

Tim visited the vicinity of the mine from time to time to watch its progress. When he saw that the lead that was being followed was about to break out into the adjoining canyon, where it would be lost, he became desperate enough to take some action. He would get at least some of the gold that was rightfully his!

He studied the movements of the guards on the sluice boxes. Then, when he knew the timing of the patrols, he slipped into an area about a thousand feet below the mine. Despite the rush of the water pounding its full load of sand and gravel against his wrists, he scooped up a hundred pounds of the material trapped back of the cleats.

Tim carried his sack of wet concentrates to a camp hidden in the brush along a creek below the mine. There he recovered more gold in two hours of panning than he had been able to find in the river benches and bars during the weeks of hard work in the previous year. To carry out the plan he had in mind he needed much more, so during the following month he made a dozen more raids.

When at last he had enough to put his plan into operation, he left the hills and struck up an acquaintance with two Civil War veterans in a Marysville bar. They were down on their luck and were open to any suggestion. A well-paid "vacation" in the mountains seemed to be exactly what they were looking for. The fact that they would go armed, and that there might be some gunplay, bothered them not at all when they saw that Tim had the dust to pay, even though his plan did not succeed.

He had already purchased three fine saddle horses and six pack mules that had been at pasture for some time and were in fine condition. They loaded the mules with enough junk mining materials to give the cavalcade the look of a well-financed prospecting trip, and took to the hills.

From their camp on a tributary of the Yuba, one of the men walked to the mine and applied for a job. He claimed to have had no mining experience. He knew that he would not be hired. He was allowed to spend the night in camp, however, so he was able to find out the date of the next "cleanup." This was important, as it was necessary to strike when the riffles in the sluice boxes held the most gold, but they must not wait until some of the owners arrived to supervise the cleanup. They would be much too inclined to fight to protect their property. The ordinary miners would not care to risk their necks merely to protect some rich man's gold.

On the day chosen they tied handkerchiefs across their faces so that only their eyes were exposed and rode boldly into the mine building area just before dark. They must get the gold and get away into the hills while they had many hours of travel time before daybreak.

Tim slipped up behind the sluice box guard, stuck a gun in his ribs, and tied him securely. One of the men threw a ten-pound keg of blasting powder fitted with a short fuse into the empty mess hall, then held the off-shift miners at the point of a gun when they rushed out of the bunkhouse to see what all the commotion was about. The third man threw a similar keg of powder into the working area and held the men there at bay until Tim and his helper arrived to tie their hands. Together they herded the workers into the bunkhouse and tied them securely. They must not be allowed to interfere with the unscheduled cleanup. They would be released the following morning when the first of the owners arrived.

Next the "highgraders" turned the water out of the sluice boxes and set about filling the twenty-four canvas bags that the mules would carry out of the area. They used a flat-point shovel to scoop the gravel from back of the cleats, pausing only long enough to throw away the largest of the rocks. They were able to fill their bags from the upper hundred feet of the boxes. This, they knew, would contain the largest of the nuggets and the richest amalgam.

Their horses and mules were well rested, so they made good time as they pushed eastward towards the Sierra summit. They kept always to little-traveled trails that Tim had scouted out in advance. At the end of the first hour the mules began to show the strains of carrying their overload. The men stopped by a small creek to water their animals and to bury half their bags of gravel. They had to make better time from there on.

They pushed their mounts hard for the remainder of the night. Then, just as day was breaking, they tied burlap around the animals' hooves to make sure that their iron shoes left no marks on the bare granite where they had left the trail, and set off across the glaciated high country of the Sierra Nevadas. At mid-morning, they found a well-hidden glacial cirque lake, one of the hundreds that dot the highlands from the Cascades south to the Tehachapis, and rested by the ink-blue water while their stock grazed on the lush grasses along the shore.

They ate cold bread and beans. They did not dare chance a fire, which might telegraph their location to the posse that must by now be organized and in hot pursuit.

They slept the remainder of the day; then, after another cold meal, they worked their way slowly up the remaining two miles to a gap through the crest of the mountains, and set their course down the steep Sierran escarpment toward the little town of Sierraville.

Shortly they crossed a trail leading in that direction. This they followed at a much increased pace. They skirted the ranch town and pushed hard to the north until faint fingers of light began to find their way through the gaps between the volcanic peaks of western Nevada.

Again they made their way deep into the forest that covered the fringe of the valley. The rest of the day was spent resting, grazing their stock, and eating and sleeping.

Tim made the excuse that he wanted to watch their back trail. He did not sleep at once. When his two helpers were safely asleep, he took one of the bags of gravel to the edge of the small creek by the camp and panned a sample. He whistled in surprise at the size of the nuggets and at the amount of amalgam that showed after the pan had been submerged and twisted only a few times. He continued to pan until he had sufficient gold to pay his helpers and to meet his immediate expenses. He kept only the nuggets and the dust. The amalgam he could not spend immediately. If he did, his partners would know immediately that he had been cheating on them.

He refilled the bag with worthless gravel from the stream and replaced it among the saddlebags. Then he slept.

Late in the afternoon they ate their last cold meal, and at Tim's suggestion they sampled the gravel. Naturally, he made sure that they panned from the bag that had been diluted at the ratio of about ten to one. He did not dare let his helpers have any idea as to just how rich their haul had been! They must not feel the weight of the gold in the pan as the gravel was spilled over the lower lip, nor must they be allowed to hear the "growl" of the nuggets as they dragged across the bottom of the pan when it was twisted and turned. He knew full well that he would be subjected to a certain amount of "blackmail" once his fellow felons had drunk up the money he had promised them for their "fishing trip." He must be able to convince them that he too had spent all his profits from the expedition. He could stake them to a drink and a meal, and that was all!

Just before dusk they rode boldly into the village of Portola, the town that was developing just west of Jim Beckworth's Trading Post on the Feather River. They corraled their stock and found rooms at a boardinghouse. After bathing and shaving, and eating a full meal, Tim paid each the $1,000 he had promised, and added another $100, for goodwill. Then he invited them to the local saloon for a drink to celebrate their success.

Tim took only one drink himself. He insisted, however, that the others drink up. In fact he loaded them with the best whiskey in the house. As he had planned, his two helpers soon collapsed into a drunken stupor. He then paid the barkeeper to see that they did not get "rolled" for the gold they carried, and to see that they got safely back to the boardinghouse when they had regained their senses enough to walk.

He returned to the boardinghouse, picked up the saddlebags, and made his way back to the corral. Quickly saddling the horses, he repacked the bags of gravel on the mules, and rode as rapidly as possible, without attracting too much attention, back along the trail to the south.

Although it was long after dark, he found the stream where they had camped during the day, and rested until morning. Then he located a spot near an outcropping that would be easy to locate in the future, and buried his sacks of gold-laden gravel. Next he threw away the saddles, the pack frames, the bridles, and the halters of the stock other than his own riding horse, and drove them well back into the hills along the lower slopes of Beckwourth Mountain. He knew that they would follow the greener grass up into the high mountains, and would not be seen again until the deep winter snows drove them down into the valley. There some lucky rancher would make the find of his life when they invaded his haysacks.

Tim then turned his own horse south and rode as inconspicuously as possible until he reached the Hennesse Pass Road. There he dug up a cache of well-worn prospector's clothes and some mining tools. He threw away his good saddle and substituted a well-worn pack saddle, to which he lashed the mining tools. The horse he liberally plastered with mud, and trimmed its mane and tail to resemble those of a pack animal that had spent months crashing through the brush along mountain streams. Now he was ready to be seen. If one did not look closely at the good lines of the pack animal, Tim could not be other than the hard-luck prospector who had been roaming these same hills for the past several years.

He made his way over the pass and down to the spot where the first sacks of gravel had been buried. These he dug up, and, making several trips, he moved them to a new burial spot a quarter mile downstream. Then he returned to a secluded spot where he could watch unseen when his partners in crime came riding back on the horses they had bought in Portola, their condition of utter exhaustion showing that they had been pushed to the limit of their endurance by their riders, who were bent on getting back to the original cache to get an additional share of the gold before Tim could dispose of it.

Tim grinned and congratulated himself on his astuteness as he watched the men stare in frustration at the empty hole. They each still had nearly a thousand dollars, which had to be spent on liquor, and on women. They would not remain long in the mountains. Marysville, then Sacramento would see them as soon as they could get there.

Tim gave them a few hours start, then he made his way leisurely down the road to North San Juan. There he visited several of the fifteen saloons the town boasted of. He took care to pay for his drink with a sizable nugget. In fact he put on a good act to convince the barman that he had made a mistake in exposing his riches. Then with a shrug he treated the house and explained that he guessed he could afford the expense. He knew of a place where any man, if he was willing to work, could pick up quite a few of these nuggets in a very short time. He repeated the process in French Corral, at Bridgeport, and at Timbuctoo.

As he had anticipated, the news of the big-spending miner with "pigeon egg" nuggets reached Marysville ahead of him. There, even though his supply from the half sack of gravel was running low, he had no trouble establishing unlimited credit. He knew that he was being watched, so he made no effort to hide the fact that he was running a little low on spendable cash and would soon have to make a trip to his "mine" before the snow got too deep in the high mountains.

He knew that he would be followed by a dozen saloon hangers-on and by several professional spies working for the large mining companies. He wanted to get a chance to identify them for future trips. Most of the followers became discouraged as he camped and fished along the branches of the Feather. The professionals, he knew, would stay with him. They would not be discouraged or fooled by his tactics. So he worked his way to a spot about ten miles below Portola on the river. Here he rested his horse for two days, then made a dash across country for the sacks of gold on the slopes of Beckwourth Mountain. He arrived ahead of the pursuit, but paused only long enough to dig up two of the sacks. These he roped to his saddle, moved a mile downstream, and was busy panning when two of the professionals caught up with him.

He knew that they knew the gravel he was panning, as they

watched from an observation point above, did not come from this creek. He also knew that he was perfectly safe. They would be his guardian angels until they learned how he had been able to get the rich gravel on the Feather or on one of its tributaries and pack it to this spot so quickly.

Again he made his way south. This time he crossed the mountains at Donner Pass, pausing long enough in Truckee to accost his followers on the street and invite them in for a drink. He could not resist the urge to show off, and he enjoyed the look of astonishment on the faces of his guests as he paid for the drinks with a ten-ounce nugget! This time he waited for the change.

After Truckee, Tim rode over the pass and down the Bear River to the Greenhorn to see the progress of the hydraulic mines there, then up over Cedar Ridge to Grass Valley. He visited two days with his family and insisted that he be allowed to give his mother the $100 she was to take on her next shopping trip. He was pestered by everyone to tell the location of his mine. The answer he gave was rather vague: "Oh, it's about five miles north and east of the place I used to work before I took that trip to San Francisco." They got no location closer than that.

Back in Marysville, he used part of his gold to make a down-payment on a ranch north of town. A ranch without a woman is a barren, lonely place; so he married. With his charm and good looks, and with everyone in the Valley knowing that he had a fabulous gold mine, he had his pick of the single girls from Sacramento to Chico! Unfortunately, his choice of the most beautiful girl was not a wise one.

Shortly after the birth of their second child his wife started nagging him to work the mine longer and harder. She wanted to see the lights of the city. "At least", she said, "you must tell me the location of the mine. What if something should happen to you? I must know!"

He put her off with the statement that nothing was going to happen to him, and even if it did she and the children would be well cared for. He hinted that a certain lawyer had all his important papers.

She was not satisfied. She conspired with the ranch foreman, with whom she had already become too friendly. He followed Tim on his next trip to the mine.

It had been two years since anyone had tried to learn of the location of the mine by trailing him, so Tim was surprised when he found that he was being followed once more. He doubled back on the trail and ambushed the foreman. He had not the slightest idea that the unfaithful employee was working with his wife. He fired him on the spot and sent him back to the ranch to pack and clear out.

The lovers had already waited too long. They were sure that they would find a map of the mine in Tim's papers. In any case the ranch and the other property Tim had acquired would make life easy for them in the city. When Tim returned from the latest trip and arrived well after dark, he was met by a blast from a shotgun as he walked through the door of the ranchhouse.

The distraught widow testified at the inquest that Tim had not been due to arrive back from his latest trip for several more days. She had thought that an intruder was breaking into the house. She had acted to protect the lives of her children and her honor!

The Tim McGuire Mine was never found!

3

Peter, Sam, and Sarah

After the birth of Tim in 1851, there was a lull in the production of McGuire children. Not until 1858 did the next pregnancy occur. Michael began to wonder if working in the cold water of the mine had retarded or limited his ability to produce more offspring. He need not have worried about his manhood. Late in '58, Peter was born, followed a year later by Sam.

The boys were so close together, and they carried so many of the same features and mannerisms that, after the age of four, they often passed for twins.

As had the two boys before them, they did not think too much of being shut up in a dull schoolroom. In turn they each quit the local school after the sixth grade. Their excuse was that they too must help their father in the mine and on the farm. As soon as they were large enough, they found work in the local mines.

When Peter was seventeen, and Sam was sixteen, they left home completely. Several more children had arrived by that time. There was too little room in the farmhouse for all the McGuires. Peter and Sam felt the pressure building up. Henceforth they must provide for themselves.

At first they followed Joe to Virginia City, where they worked in the silver mines. An underground fire almost proved fatal to their entire crew. After that harrowing experience they found that they preferred to work on the surface.

In 1877, a visitor from Nevada told the McGuires that the "twins" had gone into the desert prospecting. Thereafter the family heard no more of them. One rumor had it that they had gone to Australia to join the gold rush there. More likely they had died in the desert from any one of a thousand causes. More probable still, they had been killed in a mine accident. The mine owner had no responsibility to notify the next of kin. Men worked at their own risk, so the owner did not have to withhold the news of their deaths for fear of liability. "Bindle stiffs" came and went with such regularity that often their names were not recorded. They were given a pay number. That was considered sufficient.

Grass Valley gossip, of course, had it that they had been killed in a saloon brawl. They had been buried on "Boot Hill" near some long-forgotten ghost town.

After ten years the family gave up hope of ever hearing from them again. Thereafter their names were seldom mentioned, certainly not to strangers.

Again there was a break in the succession of children. The first girl, Sarah, arrived in 1864. Like those before her and those to follow, she survived the childhood diseases, including one epidemic of diphtheria. She did not fall down any of the hundreds of open shafts in the hills where all the children in the neighborhood played. She did not get bitten by a rattlesnake, or by a rabid dog or skunk. Then, being blessed by having four older brothers who were more than willing to come to her rescue if and when she was picked on by some bully at school, she suffered no more than a minimal amount of hairpulling, and some skinned knees and elbows when squabbles did develop.

After school, which, as with the boys, extended only through the sixth grade, Sarah helped her mother cook for the older members of the family, and acted as a surrogate mother for the younger children as they appeared on the scene.

She could have married at sixteen, which was the age at which most of her girlfriends decided that, if they were going to be saddled with the task of raising a family, it might better be their own babies they were caring for. She was beautiful and vivacious. She could have her choice and she knew it, so she waited.

In 1882, when she was eighteen, she met and, after a whirl-

wind courtship, married William Mitchell. The courtship needed
to be fast. Mitchell was one of the first of the young engineers
to come to Grass Valley to work in and to observe the operations
of the deep quartz mines in that area, and to carry the advanced
knowledge to the outside world. He was under contract to go
to Mexico to superintend a group of mines owned by a syndi-
cate.

He had little time for courtship. If he really wanted that Irish
girl with the dancing eyes, the quick smile, and the peaches-and-
cream complexion, as well as the temper that could put any man
in his place instantly, he had to act quickly. He did!

The honeymoon was spent in Mexico. Three children were
born there: William, Jr., later Dr. William Mitchell, a well-known
physician and surgeon in Pasadena; Georgie; later Mrs. Lou
Agnew, wife of an Okland police captain; and Sister Celestine,
for many years head of the music department of Mount Saint
Mary's College in Los Angeles.

Sister Celestine, along with a traveling companion, visited
Grass Valley for a short vacation each summer. On many occasions the writer had the pleasure of acting as their chauffeur (in
his car of course). Celestine loved to visit Lake Tahoe, and,
because she brought a different companion each year, she had
the perfect excuse to suggest a drive around the lake. In 1938,
we took the sisters to dinner at the famous Cal-Neva Lodge. At
that time the dining room was on the California side of the
building. A blue-and-gold line was actually painted on the floor
to separate the two states. Gambling was not allowed on the
California side. On the Nevada side the casino was running with
capacity crowds. Upon entering the building the writer insisted
that the Sisters accompany him into the casino in order that he
might better explain some of the details of the games being run
there. They had been questioning him as to the meaning of
"Craps" and "Blackjack." They were most reluctant, but they
were too polite to hurt their host's feelings. It is hard to say
who was the more startled, as the nuns in their penguin uniforms
walked into the din of the calling of the dice and the clang of
a hundred slot machines, the nuns or the hardened pit men.

During dinner the writer innocently asked the sisters if the college library subscribed to *Life* magazine? They assured him that it did, and asked why. With great naïveté, he told them to look in the November 1 issue. There they would see their picture watching in rapt attention the spinning of a roulette wheel. The whole casino episode had been staged to get sensational pictures for the local *Life* representative!

The sisters were so uninformed that they did not know that any magazine would have to have their consent before they could publish their pictures. The writer was in the doghouse for some time both with the sisters and with the family, before he succumbed to the uncontrollable urge to laugh and reveal that there had been no photographer. The visiting nun was most upset. Sister Celestine saw the humor of the situation. She had a hearty laugh and thereafter was more friendly with the writer than with her own blood relatives. She laughed again when it was explained that the practical joke had been pulled to even the score. The nuns seemed to trust in the Lord more than they did in the driving ability of their host. They fingered their beads and said half a dozen "Hail Marys" or "Our Fathers" on each of the hairpin turns along the sheer cliffs on the road around Emerald Bay!

4

Minnie

Two years after Sarah came into the McGuire family, Minnie was born. She arrived in 1866, and was the first of the McGuire children to take advantage of the $1,000 that had been set aside for her education at the time of her birth. She completed the work offered at the Union Hill School, now extended to seven grades, then continued at the Grass Valley Academy.

The academy was the forerunner of the Grass Valley High School, a school that numbers among its graduates such figures as Josiah Joyce, the Harvard philosopher, as well as a large number of scientists and engineers, especially men associated with the mining industry. In truth, it was the fourth school in all of California that offered courses beyond those normally taught in the grade schools.

A normal school had just been established in San Francisco when Minnie finished her courses at the academy. For two years she lived with a good Catholic family in that city, that boasted of five saloons for every church. It also had the Barbary Coast, which was rightly compared with Sodom and Gomorrah of biblical fame by the preachers, as they called down from their pulpits the wrath of God on the loose women, the gamblers, the saloon-keepers, and the shanghaiers.

Minnie did not see these things. She did know that they existed. They were not new. In Grass Valley, the same situation existed but on a much smaller scale. The girls no longer solicited openly in the saloons, but they were there. Stud and draw poker was played in the back rooms of every saloon, and, periodically, when an isolated mine needed an extra worker or two, an obliging tavernkeeper would ply an out-of-work miner with drinks until he passed out. Then he was turned over to a teamster, who kept him drunk until he had been transported so far back into the mountains that it was easier to work for some time to acquire a few dollars for stagecoach fare back to civilization than to walk out.

Minnie received her certificate of completion of the normal school course. Then she took the county teachers examination. She passed with the highest record and was immediately given the teacher's position at the North Bloomfield School.

That school was at the headquarters of the Malakoff diggings, the largest of all the hydraulic mines in California. There, although she was barely eighteen, she handled all eight grades in the one-room school. Some of her pupils were only one or two years younger than their teacher, but discipline was never a problem.

Teachers are born, not made! Education and training can produce assembly-line school factory workers, but real teachers have a spark that ignites the urge to learn in their charges. They have a feeling for what is difficult for children to understand, and they know instinctively how to simplify the problem to make it understandable to the learner. Without exception they lead the way by asking the right questions. The child is allowed to feel that he has discovered the answer by himself. His pride in achievement is stimulated. Learning becomes fun!

Minnie had these traits of a successful teacher to a high degree. She gave her love to all the children. But this was coupled with a firm disciplinary hand. She had the quick Irish wit to see and to appreciate the practical jokes that were a part of the lifestyle of the pioneer community. She laughed with the perpetrators and smothered the victims with sympathy and with love. Then after a few moments of merriment, a sharp rap of her ruler on the desk restored order. Then it was all business as usual.

Being almost the only single girl in the community beyond the age of sixteen, the beautiful, laughing Irish girl did not lack for suitors. Also, being of a practical turn of mind, she selected, with better than average judgment, those whom she would allow to accompany her to the picnics and dances.

The winner was one William Shoemaker, a mining engineer. He was a young man in a young profession. His future seemed assured. But only after an arduous courtship did he woo her away from her first love, teaching.

At the end of her second year at the Malakoff, they were married. Naturally she could teach no more. Married women, at that time, did not work outside the home. They kept house for their husbands and bore and raised their children.

Had normal patterns been followed, Minnie's story would have ended at this point. But fate had a way of interfering.

Shoemaker was struck by a blast of water from the nozzle of a hydraulic monitor. The six-inch stream of water was being propelled from the iron throat under a hydrostatic head of seven hundred feet. This produced a pressure of about three hundred pounds per square inch. Fortunately, he was some distance from the nozzle, so the force had been mostly dissipated. Had he been closer, the blast would have killed him instantly. Every bone in his body would have been broken, and much of the flesh would have been stripped from the bones.

As it was, he was thrown against the gravel cliff being under-cut. His main injury, besides two broken arms and a broken leg, consisted of various fractures of the skull. He lived, but he never worked again!

Dr. Carl Jones (Sr.) rode his horse all the way from Grass Valley, carrying his few crude surgical instruments in his saddle-bag. He set the broken bones in a manner that allowed for limited movement thereafter. The skull he did not touch. Modern surgery most probably could have repaired the damaged bone, and the headaches that incapacitated Shoemaker would have been relieved.

There was no insurance. The medical bills were not paid, and there was no workman's compensation. The mining company was very generous. It paid the victim through the end of the current month, and gave him a letter stating that his work had been most satisfactory. It also expressed sorrow that the accident had oc-curred!

Minnie was forced to become the breadwinner. Her teaching position at the Malakoff had already been filled. She had to look elsewhere. Only the fact that she was known in Grass Valley, and that Shoemaker had been friendly with many of the mining men and with the mine owners there, made it possible for a married woman, especially a Catholic, to be employed. The usual rule was: No married women teachers! What if they got pregnant? It would never do to have their children exposed to a woman in that condition!

As time passed, Shoemaker's condition improved somewhat. In 1886 he fathered a child, Alice. In 1892, Leah joined the family.

Alice inherited her mother's teaching ability. She taught in the Grass Valley schools all her adult life. She married but never had children.

Leah was vivacious, charming, and talented. She rushed to Hollywood as soon as she could leave home, there to join the infant motion picture industry just then bursting on the world from the orange groves and the barley fields of that Southern California location, just a long streetcar ride from downtown Los Angeles. She was successful in obtaining small parts as a supporting actress. The studio was giving her acting lessons and she was undoubtedly in line for bigger things when disaster struck.

She found her boundless energy slipping away for no apparent reason. A visit to a doctor confirmed her most dread suspicion. She had diabetes!

"The Lord giveth, and the Lord taketh away." In Leah's case the sequence was reversed. He took away all her chances for a glamorous career; then He gave her life!

Dr. Banting, working at the University of Toronto, discovered insulin. Its production from the pancreas of sheep was strictly limited. Only a few very fortunate people could hope to be supplied with the life-saving extract. Because of the notoriety of the young movie starlet being stricken, the Medical School at the University of Southern California succeeded in having her put on the list of twenty diabetics to be supplied with insulin from the Diabetic Center in Santa Barbara. Until insulin became available in commercial quantities, she was a guinea pig. She received her biweekly shipment of the life-saving material from that center. This was at no cost to herself. Money could not have bought the extract. In return she made herself available for medical examination at any and all times.

Without the good fortune of being selected for the experimental work on insulin, Leah would have been dead within the year. She had suffered a complete breakdown of the gland that produces the sugar-assimilating hormone. There was no other treatment for the condition.

The film industry dropped the rising young star immediately. They just could not have anyone on the "needle" in their company. Even if she were not arrested repeatedly for drug addiction (and she was), she would be unable to produce. No one could imagine a person needing ten needle injections each day, which were necessary at the beginning, being able to work. But, most important of all, the strain of using the needle, and the strain of not knowing how long the life-giving material would continue to work, soon left their mark on the beautiful face. She could no longer confront the camera.

Leah did not try to buck the system. She returned to Grass Valley. There she married Donald Grover, a friend and admirer from grade school days. After a few years the insulin shots became stabilized. She bore one child. Later she became a most efficient private secretary and worked to the time of her death in 1956. She died, not from diabetes, but from a heart attack in Reno, where she loved to go to gamble. Some say that at last she hit a big jackpot. Her heart could not stand the shock!

With the arrival of Leah, Minnie found that she could no longer carry the load of caring for an invalid husband and two small daughters while continuing to teach in the public schools. She resigned, and started a school of her own.

Until late in the 1930s, it was possible to take an examination given by the superintendent of schools in each of the counties of California. If this were passed, the applicant was entitled to a certificate allowing him or her to teach in the grade schools of that county.

Usually, the examination was given after two years of study in a normal school. These schools later became the teachers colleges, and the state issued the teaching certificates on their recommendations. This put an end to the county certificates. In reality only one or two counties gave the examinations at this late date.

For a fee, Minnie coached the applicants for the examinations. Her success was so phenomenal that she was soon forced to turn away people who needed her help. Later she took bright students from the local and from other high schools and conducted her own teacher-training school. She was so successful that her fame spread throughout Northern California.

Not only did her pupils pass the county examinations at the top of the list, but they usually did such a good job of teaching that her "graduates" never lacked for a teaching position. Mostly the local school boards depended on the county superintendent to send them a teacher when one was needed. Minnie's people were always the first to be sent. It was known that if she recommended them they would be highly competent.

The last of her students retired in 1962. In all, she trained several hundred highly successful teachers. The list included her own daughter and two of her younger brothers. Each in turn passed on her love of learning to countless children.

After the county examinations were discontinued, Minnie moved to Berkeley, where she became a real estate saleslady. She was already in her seventies, but such was her intelligence and her drive that she made a comfortable living in that highly competitive occupation during the Depression, when many salesmen with years of successful experience were forced to go on relief.

The one-room school building at the Malakoff where Minnie began her teaching, and where her brothers Tom and Jim followed in due time, still stands. It is now a part of the California state park that encompasses the great hydraulic pit of the Malakoff Diggings, and the few remaining buildings of the ghost town of North Bloomfield. Park rangers now protect the historic buildings from vandals and conduct tours to the points of interest.

5

Tom

Tom and Jim were the only McGuire boys to take advantage of the higher education their parents had offered all their children. True, the $1,000 that had been set aside for their education at the time of their birth had been lost through a bank failure, but the McGuire "bank" on Little Wolf Creek still continued to give up enough gold to send them to the University of California at Berkeley.

Each finished high school in Grass Valley and then studied under Minnie's experienced guidance. They then took the county examination, and each passed with ease. Then in turn they followed Minnie. Each taught his first year in the one-room school at the Malakoff Diggings. After two years there, Tom went directly to Berkeley, while Jim taught one year there and then accepted the teaching position in the Union Hill School, only a stone's throw from his home at McGuire Flat. Then he also went to the University.

As sons of a mining man, they were able to pick almost any school in the mining country in which to get their first experience. Tom, in particular, fitted into the scheme of things at the Hydraulic Mine on the San Juan Ridge. That type of mining had been outlawed some years before by the Sawyer Decision of the United States District Court in San Francisco. Tailings from the mining country could no longer be dumped into the streams that flowed directly into the Sacramento or San Joaquin valleys. But there were still fortunes mixed in the gravel and trapped on the bedrock of the Eocene rivers in the mountains. During the winter and during the early spring, when the snows of the mountains were melting and the resulting water was rushing through the mining country, it was impossible to tell if the debris carried by the floodwaters came from old operations or was being carried away from mines in illegal operation.

That the mines did operate as late as 1895 was, of course, a well-known fact. Inspectors were sent out from Sacramento to stop such flouting of the law, but the mining companies kept a stable of spies in the capital city to warn the mines that the law was on the way. The informers had the fastest horses. They also knew every shortcut across the mountain ridges, and they were not above setting booby traps on the trail followed by an inspector who took his duties too seriously and pressed too hard in his race to arrive in time to find the gold-ladened gravel actually flowing through the sluice boxes.

The law as enacted was very strict, but in order to make a case that would stand up in court, the inspector had to see the mine in actual operation. His inspection might show that the sluice boxes were still wet from recent use, and gold-rich amalgam might be piled up back of the riffles, but if the monitors were not blasting against the cliffs, and the gravel was not actually flowing through the boxes when he arrived, his trip had been in vain.

Not only were spies kept in Sacramento, but every roadhouse and every tollhouse operator along the mountain roads was on the payroll of the mining companies. No one could break the barrier and get to the mines without the companies knowing that a "stranger" was on the way up. The mines were immediately shut down until his business could be determined.

More than one "salesman" was tarred and feathered and ridden out of French Corral, North San Juan, or out of North Bloomfield, on a rail, when he lingered too long in the mining community after his legitimate business had been transacted.

The first commercial long distance telephone line in the world was strung on trees, on poles, and on fenceposts, from the tollhouse at Bridgeport on the Yuba River to the hydraulic mining centers. The main purpose of the line was to allow messages to be flashed to the mining companies that someone who might be a potential danger to their operations was crossing the river. A careful check was kept on his movements, and telephoned ahead. This was a much more rapid and economical form of communication than the previous practice of hiring a rider on a fast horse to carry the warnings.

Everyone who lived in the little mining towns depended on the mines operating even on a part-time basis for their livelihood. The mining companies knew that the local people would not harbor a dangerous stranger, nor would any of them testify in court against them. Just to be safe, however, the companies made sure that every man who might be going in and out of the mining country was in some way involved in the illegal mining.

When Tom McGuire first took up his duties teaching at the Malakoff, he was told very frankly that he would be expected to stay in "camp" until the end of the school year. He was also warned of the dire consequences to himself and his family should he "talk" after he left the Diggings.

Tom was not pleased. He had just recently discovered girls. He was desperate to be allowed to go to Grass Valley over the weekends to see one particular maiden. (It should be noted that Tom and his youngest brother, Mike, were the only McGuire brothers to marry. The other five remained bachelors.) The community said not to leave, but he was equal to the occasion. He approached the superintendent of the mine and asked to be put to work for one Saturday and one Sunday only. Normally, the superintendent would have told him that he did not need any men at that time, but Tom did not need to draw him any pictures. He understood perfectly. Tom was not interested in the extra money. He wanted only to be accepted into the life of the community.

Once he had worked even for one day for the mine, which he knew was operating illegally, he became just as guilty as the mine owners. He could be and he would be sent to jail. In fact, he would have been the first to be tried and sentenced if he talked! A hundred witnesses would testify that he had been seen holding the "swing bar" of a monitor as it operated on such and such a date.

Having worked for the mine, knowing of its illegality, he was now free to go and to come as he pleased. He could not talk!

Tom died in 1969, at the age of ninety-seven. He was and had been for some time the last man alive who had actually directed the thundering giants at the gravel banks of the Sierras and watched the "tailings" and the "slickings" begin their journey to the valley below, there to block the streams, and to cover thousands of acres of the richest farming land in the world with as much as thirty feet of stones, sand, and the incredibly fine volcanic ash that had, for a million years or more, entombed the gold in the mountains.

It is interesting to note that until just weeks before his death, Tom was actively practicing his profession as a civil engineer. He did not go into the field, but he did sit in his room and run the calculator that spewed out the data needed by his son, Carlos, in his land surveying.

His professional career had been limited to the Grass Valley area. He returned to his home town immediately after his graduation from the University. There he established the engineering firm of T. H. McGuire. This was later to become T. H. McGuire and Sons, a well-known firm operating throughout all of Northern California.

He married a local girl who bore him two sons, Carlos and Richard. The second pregnancy was most difficult. Thereafter his wife "enjoyed" poor health. This soon led to invalidism. Consequently it was not until the boys took an active part in the business that the firm expanded beyond the local operations.

6

Jim

Tom was very intelligent, but Jim, the next of the McGuire boys, was brilliant!

Jim took his teacher training from Minnie, doing most of the work with her while he was still in high school. He followed Tom as the teacher at the Malakoff school, but now the mine had been forced to close completely, so he did not get a chance to man a monitor.

The Union Hill School needed a teacher the following year. He returned home and taught the neighbors' children as well as a younger sister and brother.

At the end of the first year of teaching in the neighborhood school, Mike, his youngest brother, got a contract with the Empire Mine to cut firewood for their steam boilers. The standard agreement for cutting and stacking cordwood was $1.50 for pine or fir and $2.50 for oak.

Jim was free at the moment so he let Mike talk him into joining him in the venture.

At the end of the first week they measured up the cordwood they had cut. Each had averaged $2 per day. This was more than Jim had made teaching, and to Mike, who had just finished the sixth grade and was determined never to go back into the classroom again, it represented a fortune.

Jim was smarter. There was no future in this kind of work, even if it was only to augment his teaching salary. He told Mike to get some kid with a strong back and weak mind to help him finish his contract. He was going to school and get away from this kind of work!

He followed Tom to Berkeley. There he took a degree in

civil engineering. He graduated just in time to be swept up in the Hearst newspaper campaign to involve the United States in a war with Spain. He had been given some military training at the University. He felt obligated to offer his services to the army. Shortly he found himself in the Philippines, where he served under General Douglas MacArthur, Sr.

In 1899, Jim was released from the service. He immediately found employment with the Southern Pacific Railroad Company, which was heavily involved in construction work in the San Joaquin Valley.

A single year of working in the searing heat of the summer, and in the clammy ground fogs of the winter in the Valley, convinced Jim that civil engineering was not to his liking. He returned to Berkeley and took an additional degree in mining engineering. Then, as did Herbert Hoover, who had just preceded him in getting a degree in that new field, he found that his practical mining experience in Grass Valley was a great asset. Hoover was sent to China to open and to manage mines. McGuire went to South Africa.

Hoover was most fortunate. He invested in the mines he operated and amassed many million before he reached the age of thirty-five. Jim was equally successful in the management of other people's property, but when his own money was involved, something always seemed to go wrong.

At one time he even tried to change his luck by becoming involved in a diamond mining venture. The "volcanic pipe" was there, diamonds were to be found in paying quantities near the surface, but as the depth increased, the quantity and the quality of the stones decreased. Eventually the mine had to be closed.

Jim did build up a fine reputation as a competent mining engineer working for such men as John J. Hammond and for various companies that Cecil Rhodes had founded in Africa. His greatest contributions came, however, from two discoveries or innovations in the mining industry. Both of his contributions came as a direct result of his California experience.

Very shortly after he arrived in the Randsburg Mining District, he used his own initiative to order men and machines out of a certain part of the mine where he was employed as a junior engineer.

The chief engineer and the mine owner were most disturbed by his act of insubordination in closing a rich stope without prior consultation. Jim was in the process of being fired from his first job when the news reached the surface that there had been a major cave-in in the area he had just ordered evacuated. His prompt action had saved the lives of some twenty men as well as many thousands of dollars worth of machinery.

Such disasters had often occurred in the mines in that district. No one had ever been able to figure why the "hanging walls" suddenly fell in, or to predict when such accidents might happen. McGuire's reputation was made immediately.

In the stope where the accident occurred, Jim's attention had been directed to unnatural snapping and popping noises. During his investigation he noticed small pieces of minerals breaking away from the columns or "stulls" that supported the hanging wall (ceiling). He did not know the cause, but he remembered the folktales of the Cousin Jacks in the mines of Grass Valley.

The superstitious Cornish miners believed that the mines were populated by "the little people" whom they called the "Tommy-knockers."

Of course no one ever saw one of the little gnomes who, the miners claimed, worked constantly underground, tapping away with their tiny single jacks and nail-sized drills. Those who believed in them were rewarded with an urgent flurry of activity of "knocking" just before a cave-in was to occur in the deep workings of the mine. Those who scoffed at their existence and at their warnings often paid for their skepticism by being crushed under tons of rock crashing down from above. No amount of timbering would ever stop such disasters once the knocking began. At the first warning, the Cousin Jack miners ran, often leaving rich ore and valuable machinery behind.

Now, of course, Jim did not believe in the Tommyknockers. But he did have the native intelligence to heed the warning, whatever the cause.

His civil engineering courses at the University had included one in strength of materials. In the laboratory portion of the course, concrete blocks had been subjected to great pressures in a hydraulic press. The first indication of material failure was seen when small particles of minerals began to "pop" away from the surface of the material being tested.

When Jim heard the popping and saw the particles of minerals being broken away from the stulls supporting the roof of the working area in the African mines, he recalled the stories of the Cousin Jacks and the laboratory experiments. He concluded that the supporting columns were being subjected to unusual pressures and were about to give way. He reasoned that a cave-in was inevitable. He got the men out just in time.

Jim was never completely welcome back in Grass Valley thereafter. Science had dispelled an old superstition. The Cousin Jacks no longer had a monopoly on predicting unsafe mining areas. Jim's discovery was published in the mining magazines. The Grass Valley miners preferred that their secret not be given to the world.

In Grass Valley, the legend of the Tommyknockers persisted. It was a convenient explanation for some of the mysterious happenings that often caused children to ask embarrassing questions. In certain instances the Tommyknockers substituted for Santa Claus when something out of the ordinary had to be explained.

The daughter of a Cousin Jack miner admitted only recently that she was thirteen years old before she knew the real reason for her family insisting that they must live near the edge of town so that they could keep a cow. The reason given was that the mother could not eat store-bought butter.

The butter she could eat had to be homemade in an old-fashioned plunger churn. When the churning in the kitchen stopped unexpectedly on several occasions and the pounding continued, the little girl finally realized that her father was in the cellar breaking up highgrade rock, and that the churning was but a pretext to cover up the sound in case a neighbor came by. Before she was thirteen, she had believed her parents when they had told her that the basement pounding was the work of the Tommyknockers, who were following a tiny stringer in the rock below the house, a ledge too small for the mining companies to stope out.

At thirteen she could understand why the noise in the basement must not be talked about in public. Now she could be trusted not to give away the family secret. Before she understood, she admits that she had thought her father lazy and cruel. Every time the churning was to be done, he sneaked to the cellar and left all the drudgery to her mother!

Jim's second contribution to the science of mining had a much greater impact on the operation of deep mines the world over.

The Rand District mines at that time were experiencing a heat problem that was causing one after another to close, even though rich ore was still available on every hand.

Normally, as a mine increases in depth, there is an increase in temperature. In the Rand district the temperature gradient was more than double that encountered in most mines. (Paradoxically, there is no increase of temperature in the Grass Valley mines. Even at the extreme depth of ten thousand feet, the temperature is exactly the same as at one hundred feet.)

Before Jim helped solve the problem, the working areas often became so hot that men could work no more than fifteen minutes; then they had to move to a cool place to recover. Often one or two hours of actual working time per day was all that even the heat-conditioned South Africans could stand. The walls of the working areas were so hot that the rocks would blister the flesh of the miners if they were touched. Protective clothing had to be worn at all times. Water sprayed on the surface of the rocks to cool them increased the woes of the workers. It only added to the humidity of the air, making working conditions even more uncomfortable.

In very small mines refrigeration of the air that was pumped into the working areas for ventilation partially solved the problem, but in the larger mines the volume of air to be cooled was so great, and the distances it had to be pumped, so long, that that method was impractical.

Jim called on his experience of working in the intense heat of the San Joaquin Valley in California to solve the problem. There he had seen men working in the heat of the summer sun when temperatures often exceeded a hundred and twenty degrees.

In the mines the men fainted if they tried to work at similar temperatures. He reasoned correctly that the difference was not that the men were surrounded by the hot walls that radiated heat in all directions, and it was not that the men were forced to work in closely confined areas. The real difference was that the air in the mines was always close to a hundred percent relative humidity.

The solution was simple: Dehumidify the air in the working areas. Jim adapted an air-drying machine to make it portable. The working areas were isolated and the air dried. Now the men perspired freely and the evaporation of the moisture from their skin cooled them just as it did the men in the dessicated air in the California interior valleys. The rocks of the walls would still burn if touched, but they could be draped with an insulating material and the men worked in safety.

Many of the African mines reopened, and, because of the increased efficiency in the labor force, those that had been about to close began to operate at a profit once more.

Early in 1912, Jim was invited to address a section of the World Mining Congress in London. Before leaving South Africa, he arranged an extended vacation to visit his aging mother in California.

The boat train from London to Liverpool was derailed. No one was hurt, and only three hours were lost due to the slight accident. This loss of time, however, caused him to miss the sailing of his ship. The Cunard Line had another ship sailing the same day. He found a berth on that boat and arrived in New York only a day later than he had expected.

In New York, he managed to catch the same train west on which he had his original reservations, so he was surprised by the absence of any of the family to meet him when he stepped down from the narrow gauge railroad coach from Colfax. He had letters verifying that he was expected on that train.

He asked the stationmaster to watch his baggage and walked the ten blocks through the business district of the little city and up the West Main Street hill to the small house where his mother now lived.

Without knocking, he walked into the parlor of the house only to find the entire family assembled there. They had gathered to decide what would be an appropriate memorial service to hold for him!

The ship he had missed in Liverpool was the *TITANIC!* His name had not been removed from the passenger list, and he was not listed among the survivors!

That Jim was recognized as a world authority on mining is evidenced by the fact that President Wilson called him to Washington at the begining of World War I. There he became one of the famous "Dollar-a-year Men." He acted as chairman of the board that allocated strategic metals.

In his official capacity in Washington he met and became well acquainted with Bernard Baruch, the Wall Street operator and advisor of Presidents. Following the Armistice in November 1918, Jim joined Baruch's staff in New York as advisor and manager of his extensive mining portfolio.

In 1923, Jim left Baruch and became an operator on the Street on his own account. He made and lost several small fortunes. In mid-1929, he saw that a "crash" could not be averted. He sold his holdings and moved to San Francisco, to ride out the storm.

In 1932, he got back into the market, and thereafter made a comfortable living by supercautious speculations. Each morning at six he was in his broker's office. He made an exhaustive study of each stock before he bought, and he was quick to sell when changing government policy or changing economic forces affected that stock adversely. On the other hand he had the nerve to ride with the stock of a well-managed company through short-term adversities.

Jim never married. His wants were very simple. He lived in a modest hotel room and took his meals at a cafeteria. After he began to make money from his stock operations once more, he took from his profits only enough to pay his living expenses. The remainder he gave away. He helped support several church charities, but mostly his money went to his relatives who had not been so fortunate as he.

Minnie, Tom, Lucy, and Mike were all still living. Sarah

lived only to receive the first of the gifts. After her death in 1934, her heirs continued to share in the "dividends." Jim had no favorites. He was scrupulous in dividing his gifts equally, the only exception being a few payments to Georgie Agnew for his room and board when he lived with her for a short time during World War II. He also gave Minnie a little something extra to compensate her generosity in keeping Richard McGuire, Tom's younger boy, in the University when the Depression made it impossible for him to contribute to his son's education.

The gifts varied in amount according to how well he had been able to forecast the market. They were made on each special calendar day. Naturally, Christmas came first, but thereafter, Easter, the Fourth of July, Labor Day, Thanksgiving, and so forth, each called for a check. Also each brother and sister was presented with a special check on his or her birthday.

When the series of gifts began, Jim told the family that they could do with the money as they pleased. It was theirs. They could invest it. They could spend it foolishly. They could go to Reno and gamble with it. He would ask no questions. There was just one stipulation. Under no circumstances were they to "play" the market; that is, they were not to buy stocks on margin. They were warned in no uncertain terms that if he ever found them speculating in stocks, he would cut them off from further gifts. Furthermore, he would cut them out of his will! He meant it, and they knew it.

With the first of the checks he enclosed a note, which read in part. "I spend sixteen hours a day studying the market. I only expect to win fifty-five percent of the time. I have had a world of experience on Wall Street. I know the heads of many of the companies I invest in. Now, other than by sheer luck, what chance would any of you have trying to outthink, and to outguess the professionals who all too often rig the market? You stay out!"

They all followed his instructions to the letter, with the exception of Mike. He bought mining stock. In a very few cases on margin.

Mining stocks were, of course, the most risky of all securities.

This was particurally true of gold-mining stocks, but Mike invested only in the local mines. In that field he was the professional. He had firsthand knowledge of the operations and of the possibilities of each mine making a profit. Even with the inside information he was not always right, but his profits were substantial.

After exhaustive study of the market, Jim admitted that he let outside events influence his investments. In 1938, he made up his mind to buy a thousand shares of Kennecott Copper stock at $5. He had the money lying idle in his brokerage account, but his attention was diverted and he did not place the order. Over a period of several months he went repeatedly into the broker's office, fully intending to place the order. He never did. At the end of World War II, he used his procrastination to illustrate man's weaknesses. The stock was then selling for $50!

Unknown co the family, Jim was stricken by multiple sclerosis in 1946. On July 4, he sent each of his heirs a check for $1,500, with a note to use it wisely as it would be the last. They all thought that he was trying to be humorous. He was not. He died on Christmas night of that year.

The writer always considered Jim to be one of the most intelligent men he had ever known. Of course he had good reason to think so. In his will, Jim named him his executor. The fortune was not large, but it did enable the remaining siblings to live in relative comfort for the remainder of their lives. After Jim stopped going to the brokerage office and discontinued his speculations, he busied himself on one of his pet projects. He perfected and published a perpetual calendar. On a single 8½×11 cardboard sheet he printed a series of days and numbers. By following the very simple directions, it is possible to find the day of the week for any day in history. This applies to both the Julian and the Gregorian calendars. Using the Julian calendar it is possible to project any date before the year 1. After the calendar was completed and published, Jim spent the remainder of his allotted time, which he knew to be very short, in devising shorter methods of solving complex mathematical engineering problems. How he would have loved to work with the modern electronic computers!

7

Lucy

Lucy and Mike, the youngest of the family, were also the "strangers." They were cast from a different mold. Whereas all their older brothers and sisters had been "tall, dark, and handsome," these two showed no charisteristics of the "Black Irish." They were "blessed" with carrot-red hair, which in Lucy's case all too often got pulled as she was growing up, and with fair complexions. This kind of skin freckled at the barest exposure to direct sunlight. The freckles were not of the cute variety; rather they formed large, almost disfiguring blotches.

Had Lucy allowed herself to gain about fifty unneeded and unwanted pounds, the pair could easily have passed for the original prototypes of the cartoon characters Maggy and Jiggs, pugnosed and pugnacious.

Pugnacious, however, applied only to Mike. Lucy looked the part but she was "cowed" from the date of her birth. She was born after Mary's normal childbearing years had passed. The burden of raising the unwanted "ugly duckling" fell to the older siblings. By instinct, she knew that she was interfering with the activities of her older sisters. They in turn were not too careful in their attempts to conceal their true feelings. Throughout her life she had the feeling that she was intruding. "No one ever wanted a homely redhead interfering with their good times." She was the Cinderella of the family.

Mike, when he arrived, was looked on as the "cute baby brother." From the time he could crawl he took advantage of his position as the baby of the family, and of the fact that he was a boy in a man's world. The parents were too old and too tired to notice what was happening. By the time he was four, he was spoiled rotten!

To Michael Senior both of the late arrivals were not only unexpected, they were unwanted. Added to that fact, he was actually an old man when they appeared. Long hours in the cold water of the mine, coupled with the normal work of farming, had brought on rheumatic joints and cramped muscles. Now he felt that he was too old to accept the responsibility of a new family. To top off these feelings, which he could not hide, the two unexpected ones were really strangers in the "nest." He knew nothing of genetics, but he knew that the "Red Irish" did not come from his side of the family. Mary's inheritance must at last have surfaced. It irked him that he had lost his ability to pass on his traits! He said nothing, but his attitude could not fail to show. His feelings had much to do with the development of the characters of the two youngest McGuires.

No wonder, then, that Lucy thought that the world was against her. To make matters even worse, she was the only one of the McGuire family who was not at the head of his or her class at the Union Hill School, when and if the teacher could prevail upon them by one means or another to study just a little.

She quit school as soon as she could. She would not be a teacher. If by some miracle Minnie could get her past the county teachers examination, she knew that she would be a miserable teacher and she would hate every minute of it.

After a few years of caring for other women's children, and washing other women's clothes and dishes, she married Otto Rust.

For nearly twenty years she was relatively happy, though fate had directed that she was never to have children of her own. Then tragedy struck.

The war in Europe broke out in the fall of 1914. Otto had been born to one of the German families that had settled in the Chicago Park area to grow pears and apples on the "frost-free" slopes above the Bear River. The Germans had been accepted as good solid citizens until England went to war with Germany.

Without exception, the Cousin Jacks and all the other ethnic groups, except the Irish, were violently pro-British.

Lucy now had a double cross to bear. She was married to a German, who, no matter how much he declared his neutrality and his loyalty to this country alone, must be suspect. And to make matters worse, her immediate family had inherited a deep hatred for all things English.

All during the war, and for years after, she felt that her own loyalty was suspect. Most people in her situation would have laughed such suspicions off and would have overlooked the ignorance of those who cast aspersions her way. Lucy's inferiority complex did not allow her any leeway. She went to her grave feeling put upon.

When Lucy and Otto were married he was working in the Empire Mine. Soon he began to show signs of "miner's consumption" (silicosis—silicon dust deposits in the lungs). Fortunately he was able to get the job of policeman for the town of Grass Valley. Thus he was able to escape the mine and work in the open air most of the time.

For years he was the police department of the little city. Not until the "boom" in the gold-mining industry during the Great Depression of the 1930s did he get, or did he need help. About the worst thing that ever happened to call for his services would be a couple of feisty young "bucks" getting into a fight in a saloon or in a speakeasy. He had a quick remedy for that. He merely grabbed each of the contestants by the back of their necks and bumped their heads together until they had forgotten what they had been fighting about. That accomplished, he sent them home to contemplate what he could, and what he probably would, do to them if they disturbed his evening siesta again!

He never carried a gun, or even a nightstick. "Hell, what would I ever need a thing like that for?" he would ask in his slow-spoken, deep bass voice, when he was questioned about his ability to keep the peace in "his" town.

He was all of six feet four inches. He weighed at least two hundred and forty pounds. It was all muscle. At a later date he most probably would have made a fortune playing professional football, if a coach could ever get him aroused, that is! He was probably one of the gentlest and most peaceful men ever to wear a policeman's uniform—a garb he seldom wore since he was on duty twenty-four hours each day. But there was no question as to his authority when he arrived at the scene of a disturbance. His voice, which normally was a gentle deep rumble, could boom out and command when necessary. Most often his sheer bulk dominated the situation. There was no need for action.

During World War I, when he was still relatively new to the job, the superpatriots wanted him removed as a "Hun" sympathizer. He weathered the storm because he was a good policeman, and, of more importance, he knew when to keep his mouth shut.

The girls at "Mable's" gave him all the information he needed to "blackmail" a number of the leading businessmen of the town. Not that he ever used the information. He did not need to. The fact that he knew, and that the girl's customers knew that he knew, was sufficient to guarantee him friends on the city council. In addition he had but to remind one particularly powerful United States congressman of the many times he had picked the "gentleman" out of the gutter, walked him home, and deposited him gently in bed, to have influence on his side.

After automobiles became common, he was given help. The traffic man worked the day shift. Otto continued to work nights, but he was the "chief." He was always on call. This arrangement suited his mode of life exactly. In the evenings he toured the saloons (speakeasies during Prohibition) and the "houses," just to make his presence felt. Then he went home and to bed. If and when trouble developed, everyone in town knew where he could be reached. He did not appreciate being called out of a warm bed after midnight. When he was, the head-bumping took on an added meaning. His sleep was seldom disturbed.

Although he worked supposedly at night, his authority during the day was seldom questioned. In 1925, word was flashed ahead from Nevada City that a pair of notorious bank robbers and killers were headed south on Highway 49. Their route would take them right through the town of Grass Valley. There were no alternate routes. The day man began feverishly to build barricades to stop the gunmen. Otto of course got word of his helper's attempt to become a hero. He would have none of it. He immediately ordered the streets cleared. No barricades and no people were to be seen.

When he was called for an accounting before the city fathers at the insistence of the day patrolman, who was bucking for a promotion, he growled, "Hell, I'm not about to let anybody get shot up in my town! I handled it best. I let them go, but I got a detailed discription of their car. I got the license number. I saw how they were dressed, and I got a lot of other details which I could not have obtained if some damned fool tried to stop them and they started shooting. I telephoned far enough ahead so the Highway Patrol was able to set up a concealed trap. They got them without firing a shot. Let them have the glory. Sure we could have stopped them. But we might be dead too!"

Otto admitted that he was sad when we had to go to war with Germany in 1917. But he knew that we must win. He did everything he could in the war effort. A certain amount of loyalty to the country of his parents' birth did, however, allow him to be swindled in a small way after the war.

In 1920, a slick salesman came through the country peddling German marks, which inflation had reduced to worthless paper. Many people of German ancestry fell for the argument that, once the German government was reestablished, there would be a redemption of the printing-press money to the extent of at least one pfennig to the mark. Otto gambled $100. For that he got 100,000,000 marks in 10,000 and 100,000 denominations. (When the writer settled Lucy's estate in 1958, he found a cigar box full of the notes. Some of them he still has. Mostly they were sent to United States congressmen one at a time, when inflationary budgets were about to be adopted. This was to remind them of what must happen if we continued our deficit spending during peacetime.)

Otto was retired just before Pearl Harbor, but he volunteered his services during the war period. His work proved to be invaluable to the military. Camp Beale was established near Marysville. Many servicemen's families lived in Grass Valley, and weekend passes to the cool mountains were in great demand.

The military insisted that the "houses," some of which had operated at the same location for seventy-five years or more, be closed. Otto did this with no publicity and with no trouble. He sat down with the madam and quietly explained the situation. She left with all her girls.

After the military police got to know Otto and his methods, they cooperated wholeheartedly. They found it easier to have him walk into a dance or into any place where trouble might be brewing, and in his deep voice, which rumbled over the noise of the crowd, say, "Now, you fellows don't want to get hurt, and I know you don't want to hurt an old man like me. But, by God, one of us is going to take a hell of a beating if you don't settle down right now!"

Only the really drunk failed to be shamed into backing away. The drunks he still had no trouble manhandling. He still had the strength in his hamlike hands. He grabbed the troublemaker by the collar and marched him to the door where the MPs waited. The provost marshal appreciated Otto's help. Anyone he was forced to eject got double time in the guard house.

Lucy outlived Otto by ten years. She realized after she had lost him that she had been wrong in thinking that his German ancestry had been one of her crosses to bear. She at last admitted that he had been too good to her during all their years together. "If he had just beat some sense into my stupid head years ago, I might have come to see that all the world was not against me."

Poor Lucy! Harris, the psychiatrist, would have said that she had never been able to get out of the "I'm not OK, You're OK ego state," and certainly being born into a family where physical beauty and mental brilliance were a right, did nothing to alleviate the torment of the "unwanted child."

8

Mike

The writer must become personally involved in the story of the youngest of the McGuires, Mike. He was my father-in-law. It would be hard to imagine a better relationship between in-laws than we enjoyed. For the most part what I write will be from personal experience. Where I was not able to check the sources of Mike's information, or verify his exploits, I shall carefully indicate that they are but hearsay. The same will be true of the stories he loved so much to tell. I do believe, however, that the stories are based on facts. Certainly, there was a small amount of exaggeration, and possibly a few damned lies were thrown in to dramatize the situation.

I include some of Mike's stories to demonstrate, or at lease to rationalize, the reason for the McGuire family's not occupying an important niche in the written history of Nevada County. They did make an important contribtuion to the art and the science of hard rock mining, and to the social development of one of Northern California's important early communities. Yet there is only one reference made of them in any of the histories of the area.

Only in Brock's *History of Nevada County* (Historical Press, Los Angeles, 1924) is any member of the family mentioned. Then only three lines tell of Tom McGuire being a surveyor and civil engineer in the county.

At that time, Jim had already become a world-known figure in the field of mining, and a Presidential advisor. Minnie was an important figure in the educational circles of the northern part of the state. True, Mike was still an unknown mine worker and

dairy farmer, but, later, even after he had demonstrated that the
Idaho-Maryland Mine was still capable of producing millions,
Kenyon, in his little book *The Northern Mines* (Union Press,
Grass Valley, 1936), failed to mention him.

Kenyon was the mining reporter and historian on the staff of
the *Grass Valley Union*. He was in position to know all the
facts, yet he chose to ignore the truth of the discovery that led
to the production of more than $60,000,000 in gold. Of more
importance, Mike's discovery made possible the employment of
over a thousand men in the Idaho-Maryland Mine all through the
Depression of the 1930s.

I personally questioned both Earrol MacBoyle, the principal
owner of the mine, and Bert Crase, the underground superintendent. Both of these gentlemen admitted that Mike's story
was true in every important detail. They only smiled when asked
why the local newspaper and the local historians had failed to
mention Mike's contributions. Perhaps the reader will be able to
fathom the depths of local prejudices in the small community
as the story unfolds.

When Lucy arrived, Michael began to doubt his ability to
pass on his characteristics. When Mike's red head became noticeable, there could no longer be a doubt. Mary's genes had become
dominant. Michael hoped that there would be no more. His
wish was fulfilled.

The redheads were so unlike him that Michael practically dis-
owned them. Only when young Mike was old enough to help
with the mining and with the farm chores did he get the training
that every boy was entitled to. Mary was so tired from childbearing and child rearing that she failed to notice Michael's shunt-
ing aside of the two youngest. She was only glad that the older
ones could assume her duties once the babies were weaned.

Unlike Lucy, Mike was never bothered by the noticeable
difference from the older children. He was too preoccupied in
getting his own way. Mary and Michael did not count. He was,
in effect, the child of multiple parents. With no one in real
authority, he had no trouble playing one against the other. By

Mike's own admission, he was the perfect example of "Spare the rod, and spoil the child."

Had he gone beyond the sixth grade, Mike would have been the equal of Minnie, Tom, or Jim. His native ability to think was phenomenal. He worked out complicated problems in mining, sometimes problems for which the engineers had no solution. Yet when the engineers did solve problems that to him seemed most difficult, with the simple application of trigonometry, or with a swift movement of the slide rule, he cursed himself for dropping out of school. He should have stayed. Then he too could have used these useful tools.

Not that he was ever affected by an inferiority complex, as was his sister. He knew what he knew, and he was not afraid to tell the world that it was wrong when he found it doing stupid things.

Once, before Prohibition, he was ordered to stay out of the mines for a time. The doctor's stethoscope was beginning to tell of a small amount of lung damage. He took a job driving one of the local breweries' beer wagons. (Grass Valley had three breweries. Nevada City, just four miles away, had two.)

Mike quit when he was told to deliver the kegs of beer through an alley from Richardson Street to the home of the Methodist minister on Main Street. The pastor did not like to have the beer wagon stop in front of his house and the kegs carried in for all to see! Mike's low opinion of the boss who would ask him to sneak the delivery was exceeded only by his contempt for the hypocrite who wore the "cloth." He said so openly.

When Jim refused to work with him on the wood-cutting contract, Mike got a neighbor boy to help him deliver the two hundred and fifty cords he had promised the mine. The Empire Mine owner and manager, Billie Bourn, had not expected "the kid" to deliver more than a few cords. He would find that going hunting and prospecting was more fun, and simply stop working. The contract was only verbal. No one could really expect a thirteen-year-old boy to stick with it. But Mike's word was his bond. He delivered, although he later admitted that he never wished to see a crosscut saw or a double-bitted axe again as long as he lived. He did, but it was only to cut wood for the cavernous fire-place of the McGuire house. It was stoked with four-foot lengths of pine and oak measuring up to eighteen inches in diameter. Pieces larger than that had to be split. Even then it took a man to feed the fires that burned continuously from November to April.

The wood-cutting contract came at the end of his sixth grade. He never returned to school. Under the directions of his father he completed the cleanup of the little gold that remained on the original McGuire claims, and did most of the farmwork.

During his spare time he made a real effort to find the Eocene channel from which the nuggets in the mine had come. He learned to mine underground as he drove tunnels into the hill-sides on either side of Little Wolf Creek, and sunk shafts on the flats looking for the elusive gravel lead. What he learned stood him in good stead later, but now he had suddenly found out about girls. Mainly he found that they cost money even in the days before the movies and before the automobile. So at sixteen, he went underground at the Empire.

Bourn and the McGuires had never been friendly, but much to the disgust of the Cousin Jacks, who had sons in line for the next job opening, he hired the young Irishman who had delivered the wood he had contracted for, and put him under one of the foremen as a "mucker." Soon he was transferred to a timber crew, then to the operation of stoping and drifting machines (compressed-air-driven machines for drilling the holes for blast-ing). At the end of three years he had progressed through every underground operation. He was now a "miner," drawing a miner's pay.

In 1900, he left the mine and started prospecting the high country around the Sierra Buttes east of Downieville. He had no success. The stream beds had long since been worked and re-worked for their placer gold. The use of the hydraulic monitor had been outlawed, so the discovery of an Eocene channel would be of little value. He looked for a quartz ledge that had been missed by the earlier miners. But the "pocket hunters" had combed the area thoroughly. They had not missed any ledge that might be developed into a real mine.

He returned to Grass Valley and tried a series of jobs before returning to the deep mines, where the services of a competent man were always in demand.

At one time he became an apprentice to an undertaker. As he told it, "That job lasted quick." Some practical joker filled an old-fashioned union suit with straw and chaff mixed with a few chunks of Limburger cheese. This he pushed far back under the wooden sidewalk that was partially suspended over a steep bank on Mill Street. The joker then ran to the police with the story of having found the body of some old drunk who had crawled up under the sidewalk to get in out of the rain and had died there!

The police looked and smelled! Then they notified the under-taker, who was also the coroner, to come and get the well-putre-fied remains.

The "body" had been pushed so far back that no one could get to it. Mike was told to get a pole with a hook on one end and pull the remains down to a point where it could be rolled in a blanket. He tried, but when the hook penetrated so easily into what he supposed was well-rotted flesh, and came out with nothing but the smell of death, he quit the job right then! Min-ing was a dirty, dangerous business. But compared to this—?

Mike did not go back to the Empire. Instead he worked in various other mines, such as the Allison Ranch, the Prescott Hill, the Orleans, the Alcalde, and many others. Frankly, he knew that he was one of the better miners in an area of expert miners. He chose to work only in mines where highgrade stopes were being worked. Once the pocket or chimney in that mine had been worked out, he quit and applied for a job in a mine that his friends had told him was milling rich rock.

Of course the owners and the superintendents knew why he changed jobs so often. They also knew that he would "play the game" according to the local rules. He would take a piece of rich rock when it lay exposed in the stope, but he could be trusted

not to get greedy. He would also see that the men working with
him took only a reasonable amount as well.

This was the unwritten law of the mines. The wage paid was
low. The owners soon learned who could be depended on to
"obey the law," which said: "Be a gentleman. Don't try to get
rich in a hurry. Take a little to buy the wife and the children
something extra for Christmas. That is to be expected. But remember the mine has to pay for expensive machinery and do
a lot of unproductive exploring. Take too much, and it will have
to 'pull the pumps.' Then where would your highgrade come
from?"

Highgrading in Nevada County was acknowledged to be illegal.
In fact it was stealing, but there was a Robin Hood connotation
associated with it: "Take from the rich to give to the poor." And
who was richer than the owner of a gold mine? And who was
poorer than the family of an underground worker?

Good church people did it. Just so long as the priest or the
minister did not know the exact source of the gold it was welcome. The parishes were always in need.

Mike chuckled in great glee when one of the churches in a
mining town burned in the late 1930s. He knew that when the
church had been built in the 1870s, it had been the custom to
put something of value in the hollow center of the cornerstone
of any new church. This was to be the nest egg for the building
fund of the new church if anything happened to this one. Fire
and casualty insurance had as yet not been invented.

The congregation of the destroyed church waited anxiously for
the burned timbers of the old church to be hauled away so that
the cornerstone could be opened. However, without warning,
the stone was opened early one morning with only the richest
and the most influential members of the parish present. Most
definitely the press was not welcomed!

The nature and the amount of the treasure present must not
become public knowledge. Gold still embedded in quartz could
only mean that its original ownership was open to question. But
the main reason was to allow several of the rich parishioners to
do a little sleight of hand.

The ceremony was arranged to allow each man in turn to approach the opened stone. He was to reach in and take out one object only. Anyone who wanted to make a sizeable contribution to the building fund, in the form of accumulated highgrade rock or amalgam, found it convenient to drop a few ounces of sponge gold, amalgam, or quartz, which contained fifty percent or more of its weight in gold, into the hollowed stone before he pulled out another treasure, which might have been in the foundation of the church for sixty-five years. Most probably, however, it had been dropped in by the man who had just preceded him in the ceremony, a man who had found that this was a convenient way to make a contribution with "funds" that he had kept hidden for many years, and that had not been declared, nor needed to be declared, on his income tax returns.

When the church burned, Mike publicly stated that they would never dare open the stone in public. No wonder he laughed. He knew, and he had worked in the mines with the "pillars" of that particular church. He knew what they would find, or pretend to find. Anyway, he was prejudiced. Since the beer keg episode he had never liked a Methodist, with the exception of his son-in-law. And that Methodist was not working very hard at it.

Another of Mike's attempts to stay out of the mines ended in failure. This followed Lucy's marriage. He and Otto had been working together in a very rich stope in the Brunswick Mine. A blast brought down a particularly large and rich pocket of highgrade. Neither was a Cousin Jack, but they knew the "rules." Along with the other men working in that area of the mine, they carefully divided the gold. Ninety percent went into the powder boxes and was sent up to the Mill under special guard. The remaining ten percent they split among themselves as evenly as possible.

Mike and Otto put their share into Brunswick stock. Then they made sure that the news of the rich strike was spread around town. As long as the highgrade "pitch" continued, they took their "share" of the miners' gold and bought more stock in the mine. Being on the spot, they knew even before the management when the good ore was about to be worked out. Naturally, they sold their stock at the top of the market.

They then quit the mine and used their cash to buy the Owl Tavern. The business was not a success. They had too many friends. Neither had the heart to refuse free drinks and access to the the free lunch that every saloon had to provide. Otto's relatives from Chicago Park all had huge appetites, but they had very small inclinations to spend their money for American beer. They preferred the product of the German brewery at Colfax.

But mainly, Mike and Otto disagreed as to who should do the "bouncing" and how it should be carried out. Mike was only slightly more than half Otto's size, but as is so often the case with relatively small men, he was feisty. He was all for tossing the bums out into the gutter. He thought Otto should do the same. Considering his size, he should do it twice as hard and twice as often!

Otto erred in being too gentle. Too many, knowing of his good nature, took advantage of him. He did learn a valuable lesson in the saloon. When he became a policeman, he maintained his even disposition, to a point. Then, when he needed to, he did use his size and strength to good advantage.

The partners were forced to sell the Owl when Lucy and Birdie, Mike's girl, agreed that the business must go. They suspected, and rightly so, that their men, in addition to being poor businessmen, were drinking up most of the profits. Neither of the women had ever demanded anything before, and most probably never did again. To do so was totally out of character— so out of character in fact that the men had the good sense to realize that their women were desperate. They liquidated the joint venture.

"The Owl" still operates at its original location at the corner of Mill Street and Bank Alley in downtown Grass Valley. Somewhere in their historical collection of memorabilia, the present owners have a picture of Otto and Mike, each equipped with a handlebar mustache, drawing mugs of nickle beer!

In 1905, Mike married Birdie (Bertha) Coulton, a childhood playmate. The Coultons had come to California in 1849. They crossed the plains in a covered wagon. The wagon train had been heading for Johnson's Ranch. As it came down off Washington Ridge at Nevada (Nevada City), John Coulton left the other wagons to try mining on Deer Creek.

He found that the good locations had been staked. The gravel he did pan did not pay enough to buy food for his family. So he was delighted with an offer to go to work for an earlier arrival at one ounce of gold per day. This seemed a fortune to a man who had never made more than one dollar a day before in his life. For a time he thought that the stories of the streets of California being paved with gold were correct. He failed to realize that a pound of flour cost a dollar, and other foods would be even more expensive. Other necessities were also high in price. A pair of boots, if and when they were available, would cost from $50 to $100, and all other goods were priced in proportion.

In addition, Coulton and most of the other new arrivals failed to see that, should the rush to California continue, the addition of twenty-five thousand hungry men each year would bring wages crashing down. The rush did continue. Wages dropped to less than half an ounce by midsummer 1850, and to a quarter ounce in 1851. Thereafter there was a steady decline until $2 per day became standard in 1868. If the Civil War had not increased the demand for labor, the $2 level would have been reached early in the 1860s. Not until World War I pushed wages up did the $2 for miners and $1.50 for muckers (common labor underground) change.

Had the climate not been mild, had not fuel been free for the cutting, had not land been free for gardening, and had not the brushland of the hills and the swamplands of the valleys been swarming with game, many families would have suffered severely until wages and prices stabilized.

At times the streams where the miners were at work became so crowded with the salmon "run" that a man could stand in the running water and load a wagon with the succulent fish by pitching them out with an ordinary stable fork. No one who was willing to work and to take advantage of the bounty that the good Lord had provided needed to go hungry, even though prices at the stores and trading posts were outrageous and many of the so-called necessities were not to be had at any price.

Coulton had been a blacksmith's helper in New York state before he had caught the gold fever. When he found no more work in the placer mines at a high wage, he realized that his skills would be in great demand from the men trying to dig the gold out of the hard rock in the quartz mines. William Bourn, who was developing the first ledge of the Empire system, hired him immediately. He then realized that a good smith would be the key to any successful operation of the hard rock mines, so he gave Coulton a half acre of land just two hundred yards from the main shaft of the mine. He also gave him the materials and helped him build a small house.

Bourn was not stupid. He not only made sure that he kept a skilled worker, but he got the services of an unpaid watchman on the days when the mine was not in operation, or when all the men were employed underground.*

The Union Hill School was located almost exactly halfway between the Coulton and the McGuire homes. Since they could remember, Mike and Birdie had played on the school grounds. Birdie was a full year older than Mike, so she started school a year earlier. When Mike came to school the following fall, she mothered him through the first difficult days.

That situation was very short-lived. Mike was by nature a leader. He took command of the peer group almost at once.

---

*The Empire ledge system was first worked in 1850. Mining was carried on continuously until 1957, with a total production of some $200,000,000 in gold. After 1915, the eighty stamp mills operated continuously twenty-four hours each day, three hundred and sixty-five days a year. A watchman was no longer needed, but the Coultons, none of whom now worked for the mine, were allowed to occupy the house. Bourn had never given a deed to the land, but the mining corporation that now owned the property honored Bourn's commitment. Only when Jim Coulton, the youngest son of the family, died in 1948, did the mine demolish the house. It had become a public nuisance and a fire hazard. Some of the foundation rocks may still be seen. They are located immediately across Empire Cross Road from the Empire office building.

Thereafter she stayed very much in the background, as a girl should. With help from Tom and Jim, Mike soon caught up with with his little girlfriend in her schoolwork. He skipped the second grade altogether. Thereafter he stayed with her in all her classes, doing most of the homework for her so that she could keep abreast of or ahead of the class. He was subject to many gibes thrown by other boys, who believed that any boy who would help a girl must be a sissy. His flying fists soon dispelled any misconceptions along that line. No one near his size cared to take him on after one encounter. His fists were too hard, and he seemed to enjoy using them too much!

For some time after he dropped out of school they saw very little of one another. She was still a little schoolgirl. He was a man, doing a man's work and enjoying a man's pay. But nature has a method of rectifying such situations. Little girls have a way of suddenly becoming big girls with all the necessary curves and accouterments.

They started getting serious in 1902, but they did not marry until Valentine's Day, 1905. It was a most hectic courtship. First he was wild and impulsive; she was timid, sweet, and retiring. He had the unenviable reputation of being the leader of the wildest gang the county had ever known. Naturally, her parents did not approve.

At last her father said that she might go out with him if and when he learned a trade other than mining. He was not about to allow his daughter to marry a man who might, and then again he might not, come home following each shift underground.

Coulton went to see Bourn at the mine. Together they arranged for Mike to learn the blacksmith trade in a large iron foundry in San Francisco, one in which Bourn was a major stockholder. Mike actually reported for work. He lived one whole month in a boardinghouse on Mission Street.

That was the most miserable period in his life. He missed his girl, but that was not the major difficulty. The fog depressed him. This was no place for the free spirit from the hills. The bright lights had no appeal for him. Liquor cost too much for his apprentice wage, and the women of the type found on the Barbary

Coast did not appeal to him. They would not have lasted a month in Grass Valley. They were too jaded and obviously diseased. He found nothing to do but work. At the end of the first month he came down with a most virulent case of home sickness. He went back to the pine-covered hills of home.

Once again in Grass Valley, he continued to see Birdie. She was more than willing, but neither set of parents thought that a marriage could possibly have a chance. The main stumbling block was religion. Mike could not be called a devout Catholic. *Rigid* was a more appropriate term. It never entered his mind that the teachings of the Church could be questioned. Anyone who did not subscribe to the tenets of the Roman Church was of little consequence. They lived here on this earth for a short time. After that they were of no concern. They most certainly would not cross his path in the hereafter.

The Coultons were connected to the Methodist Church in a vague sort of way. Marriages and funerals were held under the auspices of that Church. They might attend at Christmas and at Easter. The small children sometimes went to Sunday school. That was about the extent of their religious activities. The main problem was that John Coulton and his sons were Masons.

Birdie solved the problem. She announced that since Mike could not go against the teachings of his church and marry a non-Catholic, and since it made very little difference to her what church she attended, she would become a Catholic.

As might be expected, this decision led to a major scandal in the community. Surely if such a drastic step had to be taken it was a shotgun wedding! Only after the passing of a full year before Birdie was noticeably pregnant with Marian, their only daughter, did the scandalmongers admit that they had been wrong. This they did only after old Dr. Jones, whom they trusted, assured the leading gossips that there had been no miscarriage from a previous pregnancy.

As is so often the case, Birdie became interested in the teachings of her new church. Eventually, she became a much better practicing Catholic than Mike ever was.

After marriage, Mike settled down to making a living for his family. Marian was born in December, 1906, and a son, James, in 1912.

Coming from a family of ten children, it is remarkable that only four of Michael's and Mary's offspring ever had children of their own. Of the four, only Sarah produced three; the others who married each had families of two, save Lucy, who had none.

During World War I, Mike moved from his Richardson Street home to the "ranch." There he ran a small dairy farm and worked the night shift at the Brunswick Mine. After the war he continued to run the dairy and to work in the mines on a part-time basis. His doctor would not allow him to work more than a few months at a time in the stale, dank air of the mines. An equal number of months must be spent in the fresh air and in the sunshine. He followed that routine between 1920 and 1927.

It was during this period that the Jock Whitney interests of New York spent several million dollars trying to find the lost Eureka contact ledge in the Idaho-Maryland Mine.

The original ledge was discovered in 1850 on the northeast border of Grass Valley. Between 1850 and 1875, the Eureka Mine worked the ledge and extracted somewhat over $20,000,000. Eventually the ledge was faulted and lost. About 1880, the ledge was found once more by the Idaho Company working along the contact area half a mile east of the Eureka shaft. During the years to follow, the ledge was lost and then found several times. At last the Idaho Mine was consolidated with the Maryland Mine, which had been operating on the same system of ledges still farther to the east. Again some success was had, but no spectacular production was ever achieved. Eventually the Whitney interests tried to make the property into a great producer, similar to the Empire. They did not succeed.

Although Mike had no formal knowledge of geology, he understood the theory of the formation of gold-bearing quartz ledges. In 1928, he was able to use his knowledge and give new birth to the Idaho-Maryland Mine.

The geologists theorized that, miles under the surface of the earth, reservoirs of superheated water had been trapped during the formation of the earth's crust. This water was maintained in the liquid state, even though it was heated to hundreds of thousands of degrees centigrade, by the great pressures from above. At these temperatures, many minerals, particularly quartz (SiO_2) will dissolve much as a lump of sugar dissolves in a cup of tea. Conversely, when the pressure is released, the temperature drops, and the quartz and other minerals will be crystalized out.

Since the royal metals (gold, platinum, and silver) are soluble at the extreme temperatures, they will also stay in solution until the water cools. Then they too must be precipitated.

Many other minerals such as iron sulfide (fool's gold) are affected in the same manner. They exist in much larger concentrations in the earth's interior, so more are dissolved and carried upward to be deposited in the quartz formations. In addition, many minerals such as lead sulfide, zinc sulfide, and compounds of copper are often precipitated out of seawater to accumulate in limestone and other saltwater deposits. Gold was almost never deposited by this method, so Mike knew nothing of it. He was interested only in gold.

The water trapped deep in the earth under the extreme pressures, naturally tried to escape. It could not go deeper against still higher pressures. It might move laterally to a point where the pressure was less, but its normal movement was upward. There the compressing forces must be reduced. It could only move through cracks or fissures in the surrounding rock. These developed mainly by two methods. One, an earthquake caused a shifting of the earth's mantle rock. In doing so, weak, broken areas were formed, which were immediately filled by the water, which now had an escape route toward the surface. Two, where rocks of different mineral composition and of different physical characteristics came into contact, a weak linkage was always present. Again the interior pressures forced the trapped liquid between the formations.

In this moving upward into regions of lowered pressures, the temperature must be lowered. Eventually the crystallization point of each metal or mineral is reached. At this point the materials must be thrown out of solution.

Quartz is usually the first to be deposited. In some areas where the hot solutions carried large concentrations of dissolved metals, some unexplained catalytic action caused the gold to be deposited at the same time as the quartz. In other places the hot water was trapped and held for millions of years. It cooled very slowly. In doing so its mineral components were deposited. Later the cooled water, which now carried almost no minerals other than the very soluble ones such as salt and some calcium compounds, escaped to the surface, most usually as the massive volumes of steam and floods of hot water issuing from volcanoes.

The minerals most often deposited along the quartz was the sulfide of iron (Fe_2S_3). This in the Grass Valley area was called "sulfide." In other areas it was known as "pyrite," and/or "fool's gold." Great quantities of this material are found throughout the world, usually associated with quartz, but not necessarily so. In a few places it is mined for its sulfur content. The iron is oxidized during the recovery of the sulfur. It is then used as the red pigment in paint.

If the gold content of the magma water was small, it might be precipitated along with the sulfides in submicroscopic particles. Very infrequently the cubes of the iron compound might contain visible gold. In a very few cases the cubes of the sulfides might be made up of alternating layers of gold and the base mineral.

In the Grass Valley area, the gold associated with the sulfides was always invisible, but they almost always carried gold. This phenomenon was not true in most of the mining districts of the world.

The early quartz mills recovered only the free gold, that is, gold that had not been bound closely to the sulfides, and gold that occurred in pieces large enough to be panned or to be trapped by mercury. Later, when mechanical means were devised, such as the Wilfley shaker table, the sulfides were recovered, and the gold extracted from them. Eventually, the sulfides became the main source of gold production. The free gold, while spectacular when found in highgrade rock, only increased the profits. No mine depended on it to pay operating expenses.

There are several mining districts in California other than

the Mother Lode, and the Northern Mines. Those are found mainly in Siskiyou and Trinity counties, and in the desert regions of Southern California. But by far the great majority of California's gold came from the foothills of the Sierras between the Fresno and the Feather rivers.

The reservoirs of the magma water were most probably widely scattered and varied greatly in their chemical composition. The quartz from the various sources might be indistinguishable, but the gold and the other minerals could always be identified. Not only could the gold from the various mining districts be identified by the metallurgists at the mint in San Francisco; they could identify the gold from each of the major mines. This fact was so well known that the famous bank robbers of the 1930s would not touch raw gold.

The output of the mines in Grass Valley was shipped out twice each month through the local post office. It was put into separate mail sacks and registered. For a time Mike hauled the mail between the post office and the narrow gauge depot. He had a key to the outer storeroom of the post office. At five o'clock in the morning he loaded the outgoing mail on his pickup truck and delivered it to the railroad. There he threw it on an ordinary baggage wagon and drove away. On the mornings when the gold was shipped the only change in his routine was to make additional trips. His little Ford would not carry the additional tonnage!

The gold in the special hundred-pound bags was never disturbed! It could not be sent to the mint, and no smart crook was going to steal that kind of identifiable material, especially not from the post office. Its inspectors had a reputation for incorruptibility, and somehow the judge who might let a bank robber off with a slap on the wrist always threw the book at anyone who was caught tampering with the mail! When Mike was asked if he was ever tempted to "lose" one of the sacks on the way to the depot, he quite frankly said, "Hell, yes. Who wouldn't be? But what would I do with it? Every highgrade buyer in the area would treat you as if you had smallpox if you tried to peddle any gold stolen from the post office!"

MacBoyle of the Idaho-Maryland Mine used the unprotected gold shipments as an excuse for buying a twin-motor Lockheed plane to fly his gold to San Francisco. Most people thought that this was only another way to escape paying income tax. The cost of the plane was charged off as necessary mine machinery. The mechanic-pilot was carried on the mine payroll at $1,000 per month, an unheard-of wage at the time and place. (MacBoyle did not fly his own plane.) Actually, the mine's monthly production of gold was sent to the mint by truck. The plane might, or might not, be flown down as a diversion. Mostly the plane was used to transport MacBoyle to the various tracks where his "ponies" happened to be running. The plane was a sister ship to Amelia Earhart's, except that it had much more powerful engines. Its cruising speed was a hundred miles an hour faster than hers. Never one to pass up a profit, MacBoyle sold his plane to the Spanish government at the beginning of the Spanish Civil War. Spain paid him $50,000 more than he had paid for it new. It was flown to Spain, where it was equipped with four fifty-caliber machine guns and used to shoot down German Stukas! Thereafter, MacBoyle insisted that a guard be put on the narrow gauge train when the gold went out.

The gold of the Northern Mines (Nevada and Sierra counties) was always of higher fineness than that of the other mining districts. There the gold averaged 900 fine. That is it carried only about ten percent impurities, such as silver, copper, or in a few cases platinum. Mother Lode gold was about 800 fine, while that from the other districts usually assayed about 700.

There was also a geographical or a geological separation between the Mother Lode and the Northern Mines.

When McKnight found gold in quartz, the news spread with astonishing speed. Miners who had worked the streams south of Sutter's Mill on the South Fork of the American River remembered great outcropping of white quartz on the hillsides and along the ridges south of the Consumnes River. They dropped the tools where they had been working and rushed to these spots. In a very few cases they found gold in paying quantities.

The ledge was large. Often it reached a thickness of thirty

feet or more. It was so large, in fact, that they were sure that they had found the source of all the quartz in the mountains. Hence the term "Mother Lode." All other ledges must be but offshoots from this the largest ledge of all.

Of course they were wrong, but the name stuck. Most writers refer to all the foothill mining as the "Mother Lode." This is an error. The great ledge can be followed from Mariposa County to within a few miles of Placerville in El Dorado County. It definitely ends there. There is no connection with the smaller, but more productive mines fifty miles to the north.

In spite of the great difference in size, the ledges of the Northern Mines produced a preponderance of the lode gold mined in California. Records of the mint show that over seventy-percent of all the lode gold mined in California between 1850 and 1957, came from the mines located within a radius of twenty miles from Gold Hill. It is also a little-known fact that more than fifty percent of the placer gold mined during the same period came from the modern and from the Eocene gravel deposits within the same area. Again, the 300,000,000 ounces of gold known to be still locked in the gravel banks are located in this same area.

The crust of the earth is a dynamic thing. It moves constantly. Millions of years may pass before any given spot shifts, but eventually all the surface of the earth is affected. This movement often led to breaks in the quartz ledges: the upper part of the ledge moving in one direction, while the lower part remains stationary; or it too may move, but in an opposite direction. This movement is known as faulting. It is the thing most feared by miners. A profitable ledge may be followed for thousands of feet; then suddenly with no warning it simply stops at a blank rock wall. Clearly the ledge has moved. But in what direction? The miner can only guess and start prospecting.

As may well be suspected, ledges that were formed between dissimilar rocks (contact ledges) are much more subject to faulting than are fissure ledges, that is, those that were formed in cracks in what was otherwise solid rock. The fact that different rocks are in contact is evidence that movement has taken place along the contact zone. Less diastropic force is needed to continue that movement than to split solid masses of granite, diorite, or other igneous rock.

The Eureka Mine, the Idaho-Maryland Mine, and the Brunswick Mine each operated on the relatively small ledge that ran in an east-west direction between the serpentine rock to the north and the diorite and the metavolcanic rock to the south in which the Empire and the Gold Hill-North Star ledges were found.

Boston Ravine was located at a contact point between the two types of rock. There the harder rock delayed erosion. From that point on, Wolf Creek was cutting the typical V-shaped valley associated with running water. It was at this point that the bedrock was exposed, revealing the gold to the first prospectors. Above that point the stream meandered through a wide mountain meadow formed by the water cutting from side to side in the soft serpentine. The hard diorite at Boston Ravine acted as a dam, holding and spreading out the floodwaters during the spring runoff. This checked the growth of trees. Hence when the pioneers arrived they found a wide grassy valley on which to pasture their stock. Gold was on the bedrock there as well as downstream, but the mud eroded from the hills above had built up a thick deposit, which made the gold inaccessible until hydraulic mining was developed.

The surface outcroppings of the Eureka ledge could be followed for about two miles, but at a depth of only a few hundred feet faulting was encountered and the ledge was lost. Exploring at greater depths often led to the discovery of paying ledges, but no one was ever sure that the original ledge had been picked up.

In 1927, the Whitney interests at last gave up their search for the lost ledge in the Idaho-Maryland Mine. They were almost ready to pull the pumps, when MacBoyle, then a mining engineer who was running a "shoe string operation" at the Union Hill Mine, bought a few shares of the Idaho-Maryland stock. As was his right, he demanded and was granted the privilege of inspecting the mine.

What he saw led him to believe that he could make the mine pay operating expenses while he continued to search for the elusive main ledge. Whitney let him have the mine, fully equipped, including a 40 stamp mill and an operating cyanide plant. He was to pay 10% of all gold recovered, and $500,000 at the end of three years.

Considerable $5 to $8 ore had been blocked out on the known ledges. It cost a minimum of $7.50 to mine and to process that ore by ordinary mining methods. MacBoyle believed that a small profit might be made on $5 ore by converting all the underground operations to the tribute system (pronounced "Tribit" by the Cousin Jacks).

Under this labor system the mine furnished the ore to mine. It furnished all machinery and power, hoisted the ore to the surface and extracted the gold. When the check from the mint arrived the proceeds from the sale of the gold was divided fifty-fifty with the miners. The miners did all the work and furnished their own blasting powder. Under this scheme the miners worked harder because the more ore they sent to the mill the more they made. It was a gamble, however, because the ore they sent up might not be as rich as they had thought. They might work a full month before they found that the ore contained little or no gold.

The underground workers worked in teams of four. Each team operated independently from its neighbor and kept its ore separate as it passed through the mill.

Mike got three friends—Clarence Osborne, Guy Moores, and Jim Marriot—to go with him and asked MacBoyle for a "tribit pitch." (A pitch consisted of 100 feet along a ledge to be worked vertically 100 feet, making 10,000 square feet of the ledge. The tonnage would, of course, depend on the thickness of the ledge. Any offshoot of the ledge would be included. It could be followed for an additional 100 feet.)

MacBoyle and Bert Crase, the underground superintendent, knew that Mike had worked in the mine under Whitney. They also knew that he was smart and that he could be somewhat devious. They suspected that he might know of an undetected pay shoot that he now wanted to mine. In fact, they thought that he might well have covered up rich ore, hoping that he could later get back into the mine and "discover" the highgrade when it would be more to his advantage. They had been partially correct, but not in the way they had suspected.

Therefore when Mike and his friends asked to work in a certain area, MacBoyle said, "No, Mike. Crase and I decided just yesterday to work that spot on 'days pay.' You'll have to pick another pitch." Mike did not argue. He picked another spot. Again he was refused. At the third location he was allowed to go to work.

He and his partners worked that location for about three months, averaging about $5 per day each. This was not enough, so they asked for a new pitch.

Meanwhile the mine had worked the spots Mike had originally requested. They got only the expected $5 per ton. But MacBoyle still thought that Mike knew something; so the same routine was followed. Mike was allowed to go to work at the location he chose on the third request.

At the new location Mike and his men made even less, and the mine's days pay crew lost even more money. But MacBoyle was still not convinced. They went through the process one more time before Mike was allowed to work his first choice of locations.

At last MacBoyle was convinced. He sent word underground to let the Irishman work any place he wanted.

Mike was delighted. He had reasoned that what had happened would happen. He laughed at MacBoyle and went back to the spot of his original choice. MacBoyle and Crase both said that he must be crazy. They had worked there and they had found nothing. How was he going to make anything when the geologist and the mining engineer could find nothing?

The tribute workers, of course, worked only the ledges already exposed by the mine during their exploration work. They always worked upward; that is, a drift was cut along a ledge and holes were drilled in the ore above so that when blasted it would fall directly into chutes and into bins. This operation was known as "stoping."

Mike did not start to stope the ledge that was now assigned to him. Instead he had his crew set up their drilling machines to drift (tunnel) directly into the footwall (the lower wall of the drift).

When MacBoyle heard of what Mike was doing he called him in and asked him what the hell he was doing. The next ledge was two hundred feet to the north, and Whitney had prospected that. Mike laughed at him for the second time and told him to mind his own business! He and his men were doing the work and furnishing the powder. It was no skin off his nose if they wanted to do a little exploring for the mine. They knew what they were doing. If he and Crase didn't like it, all they had to do was say so. He and his crew would walk out right now! MacBoyle sent him away while he muttered something about "all the damned Irish being crazy!"

To speed up the work, Mike had hired a Cousin Jack miner to do the drilling on the swing shift. Near the end of that shift each day, Mike would go underground to inspect the holes. Then he would help pack in the dynamite, and see that the holes were fired in the proper sequence to get the most effective braking of of the rock. The midnight shift was used to allow ventilation of the working area. The powder smoke had to be blown out after each series of blasts. When the day shift came on, they mucked out the waste rock and sent the ore, if any, to the mill. That finished, they set the timbers and prepared the working area for the next drill shift.

At the end of the second day's drilling at the new location, Mike showed up and asked the miner, "How's it going, Jack?"

"Mike, I sure as 'ell 'it somethin' 'ard in 'ere!"

"Okay, we'll muck out and timber. You go right ahead drilling tonight."

When Mike made the same inquiry at the end of the following swing shift, the miner grinned: "Mike, I done 'it somethin' in 'ere. The last two feet was awful soft! Now 'ow in 'ell didst know hit 'twas in 'ere?"

Mike was as excited as the miner. He knew, and the Cousin Jack knew, that the something soft could be nothing but calcite. In this area, when the hard quartz suddenly gave way to the crystallized calcium carbonate, gold was almost always found in relatively large quantities along the contact zone of the two minerals.

Mike loaded and fired the holes. He was almost walking on air as he made his way home. He was sure that when they moved the broken quartz and came to the calcite they would find high-grade ore. Indeed, he was so sure that he would find the gold that he stopped at the showroom where the new cars called Pontiacs were on display. He bought the first car of that make sold in Nevada County!

When they did muck out, they found that they had cut through three feet of worthless quartz, then had continued through a foot of quartz darkened by sulfides and studded with free gold! The last two of the six-foot round was through soft calcite.

The discovery made history! Mike and his partners were allowed to work until each had netted $10,000. Then they were told that their pitch had been worked out. (In 1935, MacBoyle told the writer that he hated to do it, but the stockholders were breathing down his neck. They demanded that they get some of their money back before the "chimney" was worked out. So Mike had to go. The stockholders got their money back, all right. Stock that sold for five cents per share, with no buyers, just before the strike in 1928, started paying dividends. By 1935, the dividends had reached the unbelievable amount of five cents per share each *month!* These payments continued until the war reduced the profits in 1943. At one time the stock sold on the San Francisco Stock Exchange for $8! MacBoyle admitted that had he had any idea of the extent of the discovery, he would have allowed the partners to continue until they could retire in comfort.)

The great strike led to the production of more than $60,000,-000 in gold before the mine closed in 1957. It made banner headlines in the local papers of all Northern California. In the metropolitan papers the headlines were restricted to the financial pages. Mike's name was never mentioned. MacBoyle and Crase were the mining geniuses!

MacBoyle had been correct. Mike did know something. In fact he knew two things. He knew that MacBoyle would not let him work at any of his first choices of tribute pitches. So the two men jockeyed for position. In the end Mike won. MacBoyle was the first to give in and tell Mike to go to work wherever he wished.

The "key" was something Mike had seen while working for Whitney. In 1926, he had been boss of a crew that was drifting along a ledge that had paid richly for previous owners, but just before Whitney had taken over it had suddenly gone almost barren. The usual procedure in a case like this was to explore farther along the ledge, hoping that a new pay shoot would develop. After several months of fruitless work, Mike went back along the drift to about the place where the pay ore had disappeared. He spent much of his own time prospecting the walls of the drift to see if there was any evidence as to why the ledge no longer paid.

He found a slight iron stain on the footwall, which indicated to the practiced eye that an almost microscopic crack in the serpentine rock had existed at one time. He carefully cleared away more of the surface and found that the stain extended from the floor to the ceiling on the footwall.

The next time the mine geologist came underground, Mike called his attention to his find. The geologist took a sample and examined it under a microscope. It showed crystals of iron sulfide, but no gold. The lead was so tiny that he did not bother to have it assayed. Mike did!

He spent $3 of his own hard-earned money to have it tested to see if the gold was carried by the superheated underground water, which must have flowed through the razor-blade thin opening in the seemingly solid rock. Mike had taken home a sample large enough to allow him to crush and pan it, and to obtain a sample of the sulfides large enough for a fire assay. He was delighted when the report came back from the chemist stating that the sulfides were worth $1,000 per ton. Of course the amount in the crack was infinitesimal. It would not pay to mine. But Mike knew from experience that if he could locate the source of the water that had squirted through the crack and left the iron deposit, then an ore body large enough and rich enough to be mined would be found.

Mike also knew that his newly discovered lead might come from what was originally a larger pocket or channel lying parallel to the ledge that had been followed. Therefore, when he got permission to go back to the tiny iron stain and follow it, he took a shortcut and began searching for the paying ore several hundred feet along the ledge. Even he was surprised at the short distance he had "cross-cut" before he encountered the massive new vein.

In retrospect, the geologists who examined the mine after Mike had exposed the new ore body, said that it was perfectly obvious that the gold had been fed into the main ledge by just such a system as Mike had demonstrated.

Records showed that the original ledge had been paying only so long as there had been a deposit of calcite on the footwall. At almost the exact place that the ledge stopped paying, the calcite disappeared. It was clear, therefore, that there had been a major change in the chemical composition of the solution from which the quartz was deposited at about this point. A competent geologist should have noted this and should have searched for an answer.

As is so often the case, the obvious was not in the textbook. It was not seen by the experts. The discovery of a scientific fact once more waited for the practical man to see and to act upon.

When Mike had found that the iron stain on the wall of the ledge was indeed worth following, his reaction was: "To hell with the company. I showed them where the gold was. If they are too stiffnecked to learn from an old hard-rock miner, let them go broke. I'll wait. If I can ever get a chance to get back in here working tribute, I'll make it big!"

So fate decreed that MacBoyle and a handful of his backers should become multimillionaires, although, in this case at least, it was not the rich who got richer. Before Mike made the strike MacBoyle's credit had been cut off in every grocery store in town save the Chinaman's, and the power company had extended the final date for the pulling of the switches just ten more days!

After the Idaho-Maryland episode, Mike worked no more underground. He continued to go to the working areas, but only to supervise, either as a mine superintendent or as a mine contractor.

His first position as a superintendent came about as follows.

In 1932, a real "suede shoe" promoter by the name of Jake Berger arrived in Grass Valley looking for the location of the Alcalde Mine. The local newspaper sent him to Mike as the person who would be most likely to know the locations of all the old mines. Mike did know the mine well. He had worked there at one time when it had been producing some rich highgrade. It also just happened that his best friend of the moment, Joe Murphy, was living on the property and was acting as an unpaid watchman for the owner. The mine had been closed since 1918, but there was some valuable machinery such as a compressor and a hoist still in place.

The mine was located in "Dead Man's Flat," three miles southwest of Grass Valley in the Rough and Ready Mining District. The original ledge had been discovered in 1852 by some unremembered "pocket hunter." Thereafter it had operated periodically with varied success until 1914. Then it was purchased by a mining engineer by the name of Root, who also just happened to be the state mineralogist for California.

Root opened the mine and almost immediately struck highgrade ore. He worked the mine slowly until 1918, then he closed the working stopes and pulled the pumps. He had made a considerable profit from the operation, mainly because he had been able to sell many of the best pieces of gold embedded in quartz to the state for display purposes at the Panama Exposition in San Francisco, and later at the State Mineral Display in the Ferry Building, also on the San Francisco waterfront. Naturally, he was paid a high premium for his "picture rock"!

In 1922, Root sold the mine to C. C. Julian, taking stock in payment. The stock was that of the fraudulent Julian Oil Corporation.

In 1932, the FBI finally gathered enough evidence against Julian covering his shady deals, and his out-and-out frauds, to make an arrest and send the promoter to federal prison for the rest of his life. He wired Berger from Oklahoma City for $5,000 to get out of the country before the arrest could be made. He stated that he was putting the deed for the Alcalde Mine in the mail for security.

Using the $5,000, Julian flew to Vancouver, and took a ship to Hong Kong. The evidence against him, however, was so strong that the government was able to get extradition. Rather than allow himself to be returned to jail, Julian committed suicide!

Berger had sold bogus stock for Julian in the early 1920s. He had made and lost several fortunes in his colorful career by grasping opportunities when they presented themselves. His first fortune had come from the sands on the beach at Nome, Alaska. His latest acquisition of wealth had been in the form of a rich widow whom he had met in San Francisco. The new Mrs. Berger's name was Mattie, so when he started operations at the Alcalde, he changed the name to "The Mattie Mine."

His usual luck held. He had no sooner arrived in Grass Valley and found that his mine did have a history of producing rich rock, than he had the good fortune to find the perfect miner to superintend his first work—Mike McGuire. But most important of all, the price of gold was just at the point of being raised from $20.67 per ounce to $32 per ounce, then almost immediately to $35! With the price of gold being almost doubled, and the cost of mining materials and wages cut nearly in half, what mine could fail to make a profit?

With the news of Julian's suicide, Berger now owned the mine in fee simple, (at least he thought he did). The original Alcalde shaft had long since caved in. In any case it followed the dips and curves of the ledge, so operating through it would be most inefficient. Mike's first move was to sink a new vertical shaft 1,500 feet to the southeast. He located it so that it would intercept an old drift at the 400-foot level. At 380 feet good mill rock in a two-foot ledge was struck!

Mike continued down to the old drift and blocked out some two thousand tons of ore, which averaged two ounces of gold per ton. It also showed spots of highgrade.

Using some of the picture rock as bait, Berger had no trouble in selling a large block of stock to C. L. Best, a vice-president of the Caterpillar Tractor Company. He had formerly owned the Best Tractor Company of San Leandro, California. That company had been founded by money his father had made in the early mines. He could not resist the lure of gold from the California hills.

Rather than take out the rich rock at once, Mike was told to sink the shaft even deeper. At eight hundred feet, a large ledge was found, which at first was worthless, but when followed some two hundred feet back under the original Alcalde ledge, it began to show some heavy sulfides. This was an almost sure indication that gold in paying quantities would soon be encountered.

With this encouragement, Best got greedy and froze out the rest of the stockholders, including Berger. He did this by buying a controlling percentage of the stock and levying a heavy assessment, which none of the other investors could meet.

When Best's attorney filed the papers to get clear title to the mine, he found that Berger had never owned the mine as he had supposed. He had the deed, but the attorney found that Julian had sold $10,000 worth of bonds in 1930, using the Alcalde Mine as the security. The bonds were still a lien against the property. Best would not dare take out any gold until the bonds were found and liquidated. He spent an additional $25,000 trying to locate the missing papers but he never succeeded. Pending the recovery of the missing bonds he moved the mining machinery to the Ruby Mine in Sierra County. (The now worthless bonds were listed among other loot taken in the $2,000,000 Riverside Hotel robbery in Reno in 1946.)

"Them that has, gets," the old adage has it. Best struck it big at the Ruby. It operated all through the war, and on into the period of inflation, which made the mining of gold that had only one buyer, and that at a fixed price, unprofitable. The Ruby did continue to operate, however, until the late 1960s. Save for the "16 to 1 Mine" at Alleghanry, it was the last major mine to close in the Northern Mines. Mrs. Ruby Best seemed to have been under a luckier star than Mrs. Matti Berger.

The Mattie Mine was located on Bureau of Land Management property. This made it necessary that $100 of useful work be done on each claim each year if the title was to be kept in force. During World War II, a moratorium was in effect, so that no work had to be done. In 1947, that exemption was lifted. When Best failed to show up to start work at noon on the day the moratorium expired, Mike jumped the claims. During the next two years he did the work necessary to obtain a patent. The mine and the land were now his in fee simple.

The four thousand ounces of gold are still there. By the time Mike got title, the collar of the shaft had caved in. At $35 per ounce, the price fixed by the mint, it would cost more than the value of the gold blocked out to dig it out. Nothing was ever done, save to sell the old mine dumps for road-building material.

At the present world price of gold at $100 or more per ounce, the story may well have a different ending!

The Mattie closed in November, 1935. On Christmas night of that year Mike received a telephone call from a total stranger in San Francisco. The conversation went somewhat as follows:

Voice: "Mr. McGuire, you don't know me, but you were recommended by a very competent mining man. Are you free to take a contract?"

Mike: "Yes, I'm free. But who are you?"

Voice: "My name is Smith. O. E. Smith of Milwaukee, Wisconsin."

Mike: "Never heard of you!"

Voice: "Yes, I know. But I talked to Herbert Hoover. He's a friend of mine. He told me to get in touch with Fred Nobs at the Empire Mine in Grass Valley. He would know of a good man to help me out. Ever hear of either of those two gentlemen?"

Mike: (*Aside*) "Jesus Christ. I've got some nut on the phone. Or maybe he's just drunk. Here, Pops, see if you make any sense out of this. Says his name is Smith. Hoover and Nobs sent him to me!"

Pops: "Hello, Mr. Smith. Mike has a hearing problem. He asked me to speak for him. I'm his son-in-law."

Smith: "That's fine. I need someone who really knows how to drive a tunnel at the King Solomon Mine in Trinity County. Fred Nobs told me to get Mike McGuire. I'm sorry about calling at such a time, but I have only a few days on the Coast. I have to be back in the East by the end of next week. That means that I will have to meet Mr. McGuire the day after tomorrow. I assume that we can work out a deal in two or three days. I'll pay Mr. McGuire's expenses for the trip, of course.

Pops: "That's fine, Mr. Smith. But first things first. We need a little more identification. There are a lot of wild-eyed promoters running around in the mining game. Can you furnish some financial guarantees? By the way, it seems to me that I have heard of you from somewhere?"

Smith: (Small laugh) "You might have, if you read *Fortune* magazine. They wrote me up in the September issue."

Pops: "Yes, I did read that story. You must be the man who built the first automatic machine for the production of Chevrolet frames all in one 'pass.' That should be identification enough. But we still need to know that you really are that Smith!"

Smith: "You'll get a wire from the Bank of America in the morning. By the way, have you any idea of how to get to the mine?"

Pops: "Believe it or not, I do. It just happens that I am principal of the Fort Jones High School."

Smith: "My God! Why, I stay overnight at the hotel there every time I go up to the mine. I'll have my men meet us there with a four-wheel-drive truck. We can't possibly get a car over that road in the winter."

Pops: "Just a minute, Mr. Smith. Just what is it you want Mike to do?"

There followed a conversation in which Smith said that the local miners who were working for him could make no headway in the soft broken ground of the mine. He must have a 1,500-foot drift driven into the hillside in order to get under a large ore deposit. He needed a man who really knew how to mine under adverse conditions.

Mike wanted to know if he could have full authority, furnish his own crew, and if there was a place at the mine where he and his men could live and eat.

Smith assured him that everything would be furnished except the labor and the supervision. Mike could bring his own crew if he wished.

Pops: "All right, Mr. Smith. Mike says that he'll be there on January 3."

Smith: "I just can't wait that long. This mine is just a hobby with me. I've got to get back to business."

Pops: "You don't need to be there. We'll send you a contract. You just sign and Mike and his crew will be there ready to go to work. Sorry, that they can't be there any sooner, but the men are all scattered for the holidays."

Smith: "You can't do that. You haven't seen the ground, and I've got to know what it is going to cost me."

Pops: "Believe it or not again, Mr. Smith, Mike and I looked at your mine last July 5. Mike came up to Fort Jones for the annual rodeo. We did a little sightseeing while he was there. We drove into your mine. I know what you mean about the four-wheel drive. We had a hard time getting in during the summer.

"The contract will be for $20 per lineal foot for a four-by-six drift. You furnish everything, including room and board for Mike and his crew of four. Oh, yes. There will be a provision for a $5 per foot bonus for each foot over five feet per double shift."

Smith: "Well, I'll be damned! Never did business like that before in my life. But Hoover told me that I could depend on Nobs to get me a man who knew what he was doing. I'll call Nobs in the morning. If he says okay, you got a deal!"

Pops: "Okay, Mr. Smith. Have your truck meet Mike and his crew at the Forks of the Salmon on January 3, sometime after noon. He'll be there ready to go to work."

Mike had a lark. He could get no Cousin Jack miners to go into a mine where there was no highgrade, but he had had Finns from the copper and iron mines of Michigan contracting for him at the Mattie. They were still too drunk from their Christmas parties when he told them that he had another job for them, where they could make some real money, to know what they were letting themselves in for. They were still drunk when they got to the mine. Mike supplied the liquor. He reasoned that if they were sober, one look at the road over the Salmon Mountains, and on into the Trinity Alps, would cause a mass desertion. As it was they were totally oblivious to the hairpin turns and the sheer cliffs traversed by the access road to the mine.

At the mine Mike confiscated all liquor. They got one long weekend off during the life of the contract. The rest of the time they stayed sober. They would have had to walk thirty miles through four feet of snow to get to the nearest bar or liquor store. There was nothing else to do so they worked a double shift of fourteen hours each day. During the other ten hours they slept while the smoke of the blasting dynamite cleared out of the drift. On the four-day weekend they did take, Mike again furnished the liquor to get them drunk before they left the mine. He knew that once they had seen the road while sober, they would never come back. He also made sure that they had plenty to drink before the truck picked them up at the Forks of the Salmon for the second time.

They averaged fifteen feet each day. In a hundred working days each man made $5,500—more money than they had ever seen at one time in their lives! Who said that there was a Depression on? Mike took double that amount for knowing how!

Smith paid them off in $100 bills. "Mike," he said, "that was the best money I ever spent in my life. You won't believe this, but it was costing me $50 per foot before you took over!"

Mike bought a new Graham supercharged sedan. "For his new granddaughter," he said. He would give it to her as soon as she was old enough to drive! Actually, the war intervened, and she was almost old enough to drive, when, because of the shortage of cars after the war, he was made an offer for it that he could not refuse! He had owned the car almost ten years. His depreciation was less than $400!

Mike had looked at the car in a Sacramento showroom. The

next day two salesmen drove the car up to Grass Valley, determined not to let the "rich miner" off the hook. They were the most astonished car dealers in all of California when the bargain was finally made and Mike counted out the exact amount in $100 bills!

Mike took only one major contract thereafter. Immediately following the King Solomon deal, he was called to the Shingle Spring Mine, twelve miles west of Placerville. Their problem was exactly opposite that of the King Solomon. Here, the rock was a quartzite, a mineral so hard that the inexperienced miners who had been available when the mine opened could make no headway. (The good miners refused to work in mines where there was no highgrade to be smuggled away to be added to the low wage paid during the Depression. If there was no highgrade, and no work in a highgrade mine, they joined the union and worked in the copper mines of the Great Basin States.)

Mike looked the situation over, including a look at the books to see what the costs had been up to that point. Then he made a deal. The mine would hire the men he picked out (his Finns). He would supervise the sinking of the new double compartment shaft where the present workers were making little headway. He would take his fee in the form of the savings he could make in the cost of the powder (dynamite) used. It had been costing the mine $8 per foot for the powder used. He was to receive that much. He would furnish all blasting supplies and pocket the difference. On the other hand, he would guarantee that the shaft would be sunk at double the previous rate.

The powder cost only $3.95 per foot. Working three shifts the Finns averaged eighteen feet per day. Mike's profit was double the salary paid to the superintendent of the mine.

When Mike was asked how he knew that he could make money out of the savings he could make by placing the drill holes properly, and by firing the shots in the proper sequence, he reminded the questioner of the old fight game adage "The bigger they are the harder they fall." "I knew," he said, "the harder the rock, the better it breaks!"

During the war, Mike was far too old to get into the service, or even into the war industries. He had to do something, however. He and Birdie took charge of the civilian housing at Camp Beale, the Army training camp, midway between Marysville and Grass Valley.

After the war he retired completely. Occasionaly he did act as a mining consultant. Mostly he did this at no fee. He was just helping some old friend with information that no amount of money could buy!

9

Mike and the Highgraders

Author's Note: I feel compelled to write the closing chapter in the first person. I was involved in some of the episodes told in this chapter, as in some of the stories already presented. In addition, I believe that I am one of the few people still alive who can speak from firsthand knowledge and from acquaintanceship with many of the characters involved.

Some of the stories will be partly fictionalized. This has been necessary for two reasons. First, the stories were told to me, so they were secondhand at best. Also, the tellers were notorious liars. Parts of the stories as I heard them had to be fiction. Second, some of the people in the mining country will, without a doubt, recognize their grandfathers or their uncles. I must be able to declare with a clear conscience that I was only telling a story. If I happen to dig up some family skeleton, that was not my intention. The episode as told to me took place at another time and at another place. Any similarity of characters is wholly co-incidental.

Mostly I use the real names of real people. This is true if the figure is in the "public domain" or if the reference is complimentary. It is not my intention to cast aspersions on anyone living or dead. My sole objective is to let my grandchildren, and others who may be interested, know of the unique situation that existed in the Northern Mines during the time of their operations.

Before the close of the mines in 1957, and for some time thereafter, the term "highgrader," like the term "Cousin Jack," was equivalent to a reference to one's ancestry being of questionable legitimacy. "When you say that, brother, smile" was the rule, unless one wanted one's teeth knocked in immediately!

Only a few of the residents of the mining towns now take exception to the terms. Mostly they are accepted as they are intended. "My good friend, you are an old-timer, one who had the good sense to stay in the hills to enjoy the quiet life, far from the crime and the smog of the cities."

Contrary to public opinion during his later life, Mike McGuire was not a highgrader in the sense that he took more than a "miner's share" and that he trafficked in stolen gold after he retired from active mining.

He did do, as all the rest did, when working underground. He did augment his small wage when the opportunity arose. He understood, as did everyone else in the area, that the mine owners fully expected him to do just that. In addition, after he retired, he did help a friend get some gold out of town when he was driving to the city. And once he did buy some sulfides from a miner's widow to help pay for her husband's funeral. He did very well on his investment too! Therein lies a story.

Jack Smith lived by a small creek that flowed out of the hills north of Grass Valley. He built a small dam across the creek immediately back of his house and used the resulting pond to pan the occasional pieces of highgrade he spirited out of the Empire Mine. In due time some of his miner friends borrowed the use of his "squirrel crusher" and his steel mortar to grind some of the rich rock they had acquired. They also panned their gold in Jack's pond.

Though they all used mercury in the pans to trap the free gold, the rich sulfides were lost. The heavy floods of each succeeding spring carried the sand from the pannings over the top of the dam and on downstream into Wolf Creek. The heavy sulfides remained behind, accumulating on the bottom of the pond.

As it must to all, the day arrived when Jack left this world for that distant home where, according to the preacher, the streets are really paved with gold. The widow was in deep sorrow, but that did not deter her from being practical. Mike had been among her husband's friends, so she called Birdie and asked her to send him right down. When he arrived, she led him to the pond and explained what had taken place there. Then she asked if he thought he could recover any values from the sulfides.

Mike knew full well what had been going on at the pond. In fact, he had directed several miners to Smith when they had come to him with pieces of highgrade and had asked his advice as to how to get the gold out and get their money out of it. He, Mike, had been in the mines so long and had been so friendly with the few miners who had been caught with highgrade, that anyone who was anyone in the area automaticaly assumed him to be in the "business."

His business, however, was not in the handling of illicit gold. He had a legitimate method of picking up a few extra dollars from his friendship with the miners. By keeping on good terms with the men who worked underground, he knew when rich strikes were made and, of more importance, he knew when major shoots of highgrade ore had been worked out. He often had this information before it was relayed to the mine management and to the mine owners by the foremen. Armed with this knowledge, he was able to do very well indeed in forecasting the rise and fall of the stock of the mines in question. He did not need to risk going to jail for handling stolen gold.

Mike's reputation did often cause him considerable embarrassment. Repeatedly he was investigated by the Treasury Department following the nationalization of gold in 1933. He showed the T men the gold specimens that the new law allowed him to keep. They never found more. When that department of the government gave up, the Internal Revenue Service took over. Almost every year during the mining boom in Grass Valley, they investigated his income. Someone always reported that he had failed to disclose all his profits. These were the paid informers who hoped to get a reward in case he had made even a small mistake in filling out his tax forms. Mike was too smart for them. He kept his records in a dirt-smeared "mine time book." The figures were put down in schoolboy scrawls with a stubby carpenter's pencil. They had the appearance of being the work of a careless amateur. But that was just for effect. Every IRS man who investigated him went away shaking his head in disbelief. He had been so sure that he had a "pigeon." But the records were correct. Mike never made a mistake; that is, he never made one that the trained accountants could find. He was never caught with unexplained and unreported income!

So when Mrs. Smith told him that she needed the money from the deposits back of the dam for funeral expenses, Mike said that he would gamble to the extent of $100, but she would have to give him a bill of sale, "just in case." He did not have to explain "in case of what?" If she would do that, he would clean up the sulfides, and, just maybe, someday he would find a way to work them and recover the gold that had been released by the natural oxidation of the iron compounds. The deal was made.

Actually he filled twenty carbide cans with the mixture of dirt and concentrates. Each can contained about a hundred pounds. He stored the cans in his garage in 1938. Before he could find a way to get rid of the material at a profit, the war intervened. The house was rented to a series of Army officers from Camp Beale during all the time that Mike and Birdie worked at the civilian housing office at the base. In 1942, a heavy storm ripped the doors off the garage. They were not replaced. The cans of valuable material stood fully exposed to the public for six years. Not until 1948, did he make an attempt to recover his $100.

During the summer of that year Mike asked me to take a composite sample from the cans to the American Smelting and Refining Company at Selby on the Carquenez Straits between San Pablo and Susuin Bays.

I took the sample from the cans and carried a small bag of the material to the office of the refining company on my next trip to Berkeley. I requested that they assay the sample to see if the material were worth shipping and smelting. At first the assayer refused. With only one ton of the material, he did not think that an assay would be justified.

After a short conversation, during which I let him know that I had at one time taught a class in assaying, and that I was pretty sure that he would not be wasting his time, he asked where the concentrates had come from. I told him that we had cleaned up around an old mill near Grass Valley. (That was the truth, although I did not tell him the nature of the mill.) Grass Valley was the magic word. Now he wanted to know more. Sulfides from that area were almost always worth several hundred dollars per ton. He agreed to make the assay. "We would get a report within the week."

One week to the day, the report came through. The sulfides were worth $1.08 per *pound* in gold, and twelve cents in silver!

We hauled the cans to Selby in Mike's pickup and in the back of my car when I next drove in that direction. In due time Mike received a check from the refinery in the amount of $2,160.42! Even considering the elapsed time, Mike's investment proved to have been very sound!

Highgrading? Well perhaps? And I suppose I was involved!

On two other occasions I was involved in aiding Mike in operations that might be considered questionable.

In 1936, Mike gave me a piece of copper, which he said was the remains of a plate off an amalgamation table. The original material had been scraped so thin that it was no longer useful.

Below each battery of five stamps in a mill, the ground-up ore ran over a sloping table covered by a copper plate. The surface of the copper was rubbed with mercury until a thin layer of copper amalgam was formed. More mercury was then added, to allow for the formation of a thin layer of liquid mercury over the entire surface. The freshly liberated gold from the ore, being heavier than the mercury or the copper amalgam, was trapped as the mixture of water, sand, sulfides, and gold passed over the table.

Periodically, the battery was closed down and the mill men, using putty knives, scraped the resulting gold amalgam from the surface of the plates. Some copper came off with the gold. The mixture was then put into a retort, where the mercury was vaporized. It was then condensed and reused in the mill. The copper was oxidized and was lost in the slag when the gold was cast into bars.

Eventually the quarter-inch copper plate became so thin that holes developed. It then had to be discarded. Not all of the gold amalgam could be recovered by scraping. The plate still contained about half an ounce of pure gold per pound of copper.

Someone had given Mike a piece of the used plate, which presumably he had smuggled out of a mill. Mike asked me, as a chemist, to recover the gold for him. That presented no problem. I got rid of the copper and turned back about three ounces of gold. He said that he in turn gave it to the mill man, to whom he had owed a favor.

The third episode was even more remotely connected to highgrading on my part.

In 1949, Mike was going to Sacramento and was giving a friend a ride as far as Folsom. I was asked to do the driving. At the south end of the dams, which was the source of the power for operating the world's first alternating current commercial generator, the dam that formed the bridge across the American River at Folsom, we stopped and our passenger got out.

He had put a paper bag on the floor of the car under the driver's seat. When he approached the door on my side of the car, I reached under the seat to hand the bag to him.

I had the surprise of my life! In my awkward position, I could not move it! The content of the bag was only a one-quart milk carton. It could contain nothing but GOLD! Later I calculated that it weighed in excess of seventy pounds.

I gave Mike hell for getting me involved: "How would it look for a schoolteacher to get caught transporting highgrade?" I could disclaim any knowledge of the gold to my dying day, but not a soul would believe a word of it. Mike just laughed. "No problem. The T men gave up on me years ago. I haven't been stopped since years before the war. They never did find anything then. Besides, you should have known better than to be so helpful. You knew he was a 'tribit' miner from the Empire. Those bastards have been stealing the mine blind.

"Actually what they steal is already half their own, but it's cheaper for them to give the highgrade gold buyer his cut than to split with the mine. Besides, they don't have to pay income tax when they highgrade it."

During the first ninety-eight years of its operation, the Empire mine had never used the tribute system. It had always made money paying the workmen the going wage. In 1947, however, two things made a change of policy necessary. First, mining costs had risen so much that only rich ore could be mined at a profit, and the only rich ore still readily available was in the stulls, or columns of ore that had been left to support the hanging walls in the stopes. Day's pay men would not work in the dangerous areas if the supporting pillars were removed. Under the tribute, or share-equally system, competent miners would work there. They knew what precautions had to be taken. Given a free hand, they could more than double their wages, and the mine would do equally well.

Many old-time miners did return to take out the stulls they had left thirty or forty years before. In some cases the mine itself did not know of their existence. Proper records and maps had not been kept. In addition, many of the old-timers remembered hiding powder boxes full of highgrade in the hope that someday they could get back into the mine as tribute workers. Then they would get at least half the value of their hidden treasure. Such a chance had now developed.

But the main reason the mines had adopted the tribute system was that the Miners, Mill, and Smelters Union, was having some success in organizing the Grass Valley Mine workers. The union, if successful, would demand that the gold miners be paid the same wage as that paid by the copper mines, which were operating under government subsidy. This would mean that the hourly wage would be more than tripled. The mines had only one buyer for their product. They were forced to sell at a fixed price. They could pay no higher wages. Thus came the ploy of using the tribute worker, who could not be unionized.

It is interesting to note that just before the mines closed completely in 1957, notices were posted on the mine bulletin boards stating that if any man knew of any hidden highgrade underground, he could bring it up. No questions would be asked. The pumps were about to be pulled. It would be a shame to let the gold be lost for all time! There is no record of how much, if any, rich quartz was brought up under the promise of immunity. We do know, however, that if any was turned over, the management kept its word. There were no prosecutions.

The mention of escaping income tax brings to mind Mike's favorite story.

As he told it, the Bank of America sent one of their bright men to manage its branch in one of the gold-mining towns. The mines in that area were noted for the production of a large amount of highgrade ore.

The episode took place during the worst part of the Depression, so the young banker was surprised to find that there was not a suitable house in town that he could rent.

He approached the manager of the Chamber of Commerce with a plea for help, only to be told that the situation was not unusual. There was no Depression in the Mother Lode. Every rental property in town had a long waiting list.

At last he remembered that the underground superintendent of the richest mine in the area was leaving that day for a long-deserved vacation. Perhaps he could get the superintendent's house on a temporary basis.

The superintendent and the mine that owned the house were both agreeable, so the banker breathed a sigh of relief and moved in.

A week later, the Chamber of Commerce man was surprised when the banker returned and begged him to find some other place for him to live. There just was nothing else. The superintendent's house was one of the best in town. Nothing else like it was for rent at any price.

The banker explained that he was not dissatisfied with the house. It was much nicer than anything he had expected, but he could not get any sleep at night. It was affecting his work. He would just have to move.

"Why," he said, "I only get to sleep after a hard day's work and an evening meeting, when some crazy guy starts whistling under my bedroom window. When I ask him what he wants, he says that he has a package for me, and that I had locked the basement door. I tell him to put the package on the porch and I'll take care of it in the morning. I just get back into bed and start to drop off, when another damned fool comes along and we go through the same thing again!"

"What's in the packages?"

"I don't know. Looks like a lot of white rock with yellow specks sticking out of it. But it's awful heavy!"

"My God! You mean you don't know about highgrade? The superintendent must have forgotten to tell the stopers that he was going on a vacation. You leave the basement door stand open from now on. You won't be bothered again. It's perfectly safe. We haven't had a burglary here in ten years.

"Those miners know what they are doing. And if you are smart, and if you want to keep your job in this town, you better damned well keep your mouth shut. The real owner of that house happens to carry the largest cash balance in the various branches of your bank of any man in the state. I doubt very much that you would keep your job very long if you talk about this."

The Chamber of Commerce man knew what was going on. The owner of that particular mine was in a very high income tax bracket. In fact the preceding year he had paid the second highest individual tax in the state of California. Now he had found that it was cheaper for him to steal his own gold and sell it through the black market than to send it to the mint, where the amount became public information. Only the gold from the lowgrade ore and the sulfides went to the mint. It was sufficient to pay the operating expenses of the mine. The rich rock was handled separately. It represented most of the profits from the mine. The mine owner had found a way to keep a larger proportion of that in his own pocket.

(Thirty-five years later I got into serious trouble with this story. I had assumed that the principals were long since dead. In any case, I had used fictitious names, and had put the location at least a hundred miles from where it actually took place. I told the story at a section of the State Historical Society. Much to

my amazement and chagrin, the superintendent who had cooperated with the mine owner was in the audience. By this time
he had become a very powerful political figure in the old mining
country. I paid dearly for my lack of caution. But that is another
story.)

Mike had an endless series of stories of highgrade and highgraders. When I first met him I thought his Irish sense of humor,
and his love for the dramatic, had led him to color the episodes
and exaggerate the amounts of gold taken. Later, I found that
the old saw about "truth being stranger than fiction" was most
applicable here. Over the years, I have been able to double check,
and I have found that every story was based on a true happening.
The amount of gold taken may have been expanded in the telling,
and the number of people involved multiplied, but the authorities who verified the tales usually led me to believe that Mike
had erred on the side of conservatism.

One of Mike's stories illustrates the attitude of the community
regarding highgrading far better than a whole book of facts and
figures could ever do.

Jim Higgins was caught as he came off shift at the Empire
with his lunch bucket half full of beautiful gold-studded quartz.
Usually the mine would have confiscated the gold and fired him
on the spot. Nothing more would have been said of the incident.
This time, however, the amount was so large that the management thought that he must be punished. They must make an
example of him. He had broken the "code."

Even though he had been caught with the evidence in his
possession, he demanded a jury trial.

Both he and his counsel knew that it would be impossible to
impanel a jury of twelve men who would all be free of any taint
of this kind of lawbreaking. At least some of their relatives had
been just as guilty as Jim. They could be depended on to find
some excuse for bringing in a verdict of not guilty.

All of the preliminaries of the trial passed without incident.
The mine guard who had caught Jim testified that he had indeed
found highgrade rock in the lunch bucket. Bill Parsons, who was
known to be able to identify any specimen rock as to which mine

it had come from, and most usually he could even tell from which level it had been taken, swore that the evidence had come from the three-thousand level of the Empire.

The prosecuting attorney then held up some of the rock for the jury to see. Some of those "gentlemen" declared that their eyesight was poor. They needed to see the evidence more closely.

The court obliged. The broken rock was put in a hat and passed around. Each juror in turn picked up several pieces of the rock and examined it closely. When the twelfth juror handed the hat back to the bailiff, the officer looked surprised and asked for a quick conference with the judge. Twelve pieces of the rock were missing!

Judge Jones looked at the jury for a moment, then he said, "Gentlemen, I'm going to pass that hat around again. Those twelve pieces of highgrade had damned well better be back in there when I count them, or by God, you're all going to spend ten days in jail for contempt of court!"

The judge got the gold back, but the jury brought in a verdict of not guilty. They preferred to believe Jim's story that he had been framed. The foreman had ordered the guard to plant the gold on him to get him fired!

He had no answer when he was asked why he had not noticed that the lunch bucket had suddenly increased some twenty pounds in weight. He did not need one. Friends in the jury box are always a much better defense than the best of logic.

Mike always relished a story that cast the mine management in an unfavorable light. In part, this was due to the fact that he had seen so many damned fools trying to run a mine with no knowledge of what should be done. His experience had been that almost any man with a hole in the ground that showed some colors, immediately became an expert. True, the rawest amateur miner can see just as far through the rock as can the most competent geologist, or even the most experienced miner, but long years of following the elusive veins under the most adverse conditions gave many an old miner an insight into the whims of nature, which the man with the money, or with the education, could not possibly possess.

Too many times Mike had tried to give the mine manager the benefit of his years of experience and his knowledge of the local conditions, only to have his advice spurned, often with the most disastrous results. So when he got a chance to laugh at the expense of the highly paid management personnel, he took full advantage of the situation.

During the years before he located the long-lost ledge in the Idaho-Maryland Mine, he had used his own initiative in the Brunswick Mine and later in the Empire Mine, and had been able to locate new pay shoots in ground that the geologists said had been worked out. He was never given any credit for the discovery. It had always been the mine manager or the geologist who had "looked through the rock," and they had told the miners where to dig. Mike and the other miners got nothing except the satisfaction of a job well done, and possibly their share of the highgrade.

Mike's story of Kurt Barr, is a classic.

Kurt was the superintendent of a rather large mine in the Mother Lode country. He had been educated in England, where he had picked up many of the traditional English customs. He always dressed for dinner, and he always took a brisk horseback ride in the morning.

One bright spring morning in 1900, Kurt was passed on the trail through the parklike California foothills by a girl on a runaway horse. True to tradition, Kurt put spurs to his horse and was quick to race alongside the girl on the unruly mount. He grabbed the bridle, stopped the horse, and eased the frightened girl to the ground.

Linda—Linda Lee—was most grateful. She half fell from the saddle and collapsed on the ground for a moment with just the right number of tears. Finally she controlled herself and expressed her gratitude by throwing her arms around her savior's neck and giving him a warm kiss on the cheek.

Kurt was duly impressed by her charm and her beauty. He was not one to let an opportunity pass. True, he was a happily married man, and Mrs. Barr was a charming, educated lady, but ladies in their mid-forties living in a small town in 1900 did not affect even a little glamour. Her time was taken up by the church and the literary society. She would never think of using even a tinge of lipstick or the tiny bit of rouge worn by this radiant girl. In addition, the faint aroma of her expensive perfume was the first Kurt had experienced since his school holidays in Paris.

To say that Kurt was smitten would be a gross understatement.

The next morning, Kurt kept his horse at a walk, but his heart was soon pounding faster than the hoofbeats of the now well-controlled horse, which cantered along the bridal trail to overtake him.

Yes, he rode along this trail almost every morning. No, he would not be hampered by her riding along!

No, he was not familiar with the New York stage, so he was not in disgrace for failing to recognize the star of *The Great Pretender*.

Yes, she was going to be here for some time. She had just completed a long run on Broadway. She was completely exhausted. She had come to this marvelous place to hide away until she had fully recovered.

Her father had been in this area in the 1850s, but he had tired of the rough life of the miner. He had returned to the East, where she had been the product of a very late marriage. She had never seen the West before. She could not understand how her father could have left such a beautiful place!

The morning rides soon became the great event of each day. She had never expected to meet such a charming gentleman in this isolated place. She was completely captivated. She was also captivating! Of course, Kurt was a married man with a nice family, but, after all, she was an actress, and ladies of the stage in that day were, by reputation, at least, quite naughty.

It was also the day of the double standard. Kurt's conscience did not bother him when it became a daily occurrence for them to dismount and spend a few intimate minutes on the soft mat of pine needles in a secluded glade.

After some six weeks of these delightful trysts, Linda appeared quite distressed when she joined him for one of their usual morning rides. After just the right amount of urging on Kurt's part, she appealed to him for a job for her brother. He had recently lost his latest position, his fifth in only two years. Added to this, his health was so poor that the type of work he could do was limited.

Kurt laughed at her worries and had her send for her brother, assuring her that he would be able to find the kind of work he could do in his office. Ben, when he arrived, proved to be hopelessly incapable of doing any of the tasks assigned to him. It took an experienced man a week to straighten out the errors he made the first day. Because of his dry cough, he could not work underground, nor could he work in the mill because of the dampness there. He knew nothing of any trade. As a last resort he was put to work preparing ore samples in the assay office.

In the assay office, the men did much more than test the ore from the ledges to make sure that it was worth milling. They also tested the tailings as they left the mill to be sure that all the gold the ore had contained was recovered. The most important operation in the assay office from Ben's viewpoint was the retorting of the amalgam to separate the mercury from the gold, and the melting of the sponge gold to be cast into bars to be sent to the mint.

Ben worked in the assay office for six months before the company was able to trace the $50,000 shortage between the weight of the amalgam coming in from the mill and the weight of the gold that their experience told them they should recover from it.

Had the amount been less, Kurt would have fired the thief and would have charged the loss up to experience. As it was, he offered to forget the matter if Ben would return the gold and leave town. Ben laughed and dared Kurt to have him arrested and try to prove his guilt.

Because the amount was so large, and because Ben was an outsider, with no possibility of having a "cousin" on the jury, Kurt decided that he must make an example of him.

The morning after Ben's arrest, Linda failed to join Kurt on the usual morning ride. Kurt knew that she would be very upset. She appeared to be unusually fond of her brother. She had often told Kurt of her worries about his troubles. She was his only relative, and, as his older sister, she felt that she had a responsibility for him. Therefore, Kurt was not surprised when she came to his office, although they had a firm agreement that she would never disturb him, especially not at his work. He began to explain how sorry he was, but that his hands were tied. There was no doubt of the guilt. Ben had been caught leaving the assay office with the fraction of a gold bar that had remained after a melt. This was supposed to have been put in the safe until the next melt and shipment.

Linda was more than upset. She was very angry. She snapped, "Mr. Barr, I demand that you withdraw your charges against my brother immediately!"

Kurt was puzzled by her attitude. He had expected her to be filled with remorse and offer to help recover the gold especially after he assured her that the matter was out of his hands and in jurisdiction of the courts. "Ben would be better off to surrender the gold and ask the court for mercy."

"Mr. Barr," Linda snapped again, "you had better drop the charges against Ben. You see he is not my brother. He is my husband!"

What chance had Kurt with a wronged husband on the stand pleading "frameup"!

The charges were dropped. Linda and Ben enjoyed a leisurely trip back to New York by way of Hong Kong, Suez, Paris, and London!

With the advent of the automobile the wants and the tastes of the miners demanded that they take a higher percentage of the gold they uncovered. This forced the mines to hire security guards to check as much of the loss as possible. As could be expected the hiring of the guards led to the development of a constant "war" between the management and the workers. Any new wrinkle to get the gold out of the mines and into the hands of the illicit gold buyer or directly to the mint became a closely guarded secret. Until a new method was found, or the old one discovered and made public, no one talked. Once the leak had been plugged, there was no longer any need for secrecy. Now the town had a good bellylaugh at the expense of the management. They celebrated the success of the perpetrator, who they knew would most likely receive no punishment other than being barred from working in the highgrade mines thereafter. Sometimes he could "care less." He would be able to retire and live in the sunshine thereafter.

(It must be understood that this attitude of taking all one could get away with developed only after gold was nationalized in 1933. Before that time it was a "gentleman's game." Thereafter it was "war" because the federal government took the policing duties away from the immediate mining property. The government also prosecuted at the trial of any one caught with illicit gold. When a highgrader was caught it was no longer a farce. The federal courts handed out stiff sentences. This made highgrading dangerous. The miners resented the "feds" interfering with their private affairs. Only they called it "free enterprise." From then on, if you were going to highgrade, you had better take all you could get, and get out before you were caught!)

The case of Jim Higgins was an example of the use of ingenuity to make for a more equitable distribution of the wealth of the mines!

Any story of the highgraders must include the story of the "Blind Mules."

Herbert Hoover was indirectly responsible for the Blind Mules! Had the sob sisters and the do-gooders of the day known of his connection with the fate of the dumb beasts, the outcry over his so-called responsibility for the Great Depression would have been muted. Nothing would have taken precedence over the cruelty practiced on man's faithful helpers.

Billie Bourn, owner of the Empire Mine in Grass Valley, had groomed his nephew, George Starr, to assume the management of the rich mine. Starr introduced many innovations in the art of hard rock mining. By the year 1914, he in turn had reached the time of retirement. In looking for the best man to occupy his place, he remembered that a student from Stanford had worked for him during one of his summer vacations and had for a time become the engineer at the Sneath-Clay Mine, which was located only five miles north of the Empire. Surely, he thought, Hoover must be tired of wandering all over the earth. He must be ready to settle down to a routine job where he could live in the almost perpetual sunshine of the Sierra foothills.

Hoover thanked him for the offer, but said, "get Fred Nobs."

Nobs had been a classmate of Hoover's at Stanford. They were personal friends and had worked on many projects together.

So, Starr retired in 1915, and Nobs moved into the "cottage" just north of the Irish manor house that Bourn had built on the hill overlooking the mine that had brought him his great fortune.

The cottage still stands, as does the "Bourn Mansion." Mrs. Nobs, Fred's widow, still occupies the modest home, but the "Mansion" stands empty and alone to watch over the surrounding park and the Empire Tennis Club, where the elite of Northern California once gathered to mingle with the great and the near great.

The war in Europe had already created an insatiable demand for copper from the mines of the world. The mines of the Great Basin in the western United States were offering double wages for experienced miners. Nobs realized that if he was to keep the mine open he must make more efficient use of his limited labor supply. Hence the mules.

The idea of replacing the one-man, one-car operation with a train of cars pulled by a mule was not new, but the deep quartz mines had a seemingly insurmountable problem. The shafts leading to the underground workings were small and crooked. There was no way to get the mules to the working areas.

Some mines had sent down Shetland ponies. They helped for a time, but they could not survive for more than a few months in the cold, damp darkness. The tougher mules had been used the world over where adits (tunnels) formed the egress for the working areas. These openings were always large enough to allow the mules to walk in and eventually to walk out again at the end of their useful life.

The Grass Valley mines were already working at the four-thousand-foot level. The idea of enlarging the shafts was patently impractical. Nobs had a better idea.

He had once visited the tin mines of Cornwall and the coal mines of Wales. There he had seen the Welsh ponies working in the mines. He knew that they had to leave the mines at the end of each working day to be stabled in the fresh air. Otherwise they contracted pneumonia and died within a few weeks. Why not, Nobs thought, cross the small Welsh mares with the smallest Jacks he could find, and get a mule small enough to to be lowered into the deepest part of the mine?

Fortunately, a pony ranch in the Sacramento Valley had a few Welsh mares. Nobs had no trouble getting the owner to find a small Jack. The mine guaranteed to buy the first dozen of the "get."

Yearling mules were restrained in a specially prepared canvas bag and lowered into the mine, where stables had already been prepared at the four-thousand- foot level. At the age of eighteen months the mules were harnessed and put to work. They were an immediate success. Only one difficulty marred the experiment. The young mules continued to grow. At maturity, although not much larger than a large burro, they did reach a size too great to allow them to be brought to the surface until death made it possible to truss them into an unnatural shape to fit into the limited area of an ore skip.

When rich ledges were later found below the four-thousand-foot level, the shafts leading down were made much larger. They were also sunk vertically or at such a steep incline that elevator cages could now be used to raise and to lower the men, mules, ore, and mining materials.

The mature mules hauled a train of as many as ten cars. Their working day of ten hours was the same as that of the miners. After 1920, when the men's hours were cut to eight, the mules also got the added time off.

Once underground they saw no more light save the dim flicker of the miners' carbide lamps in the drifts (tunnels), and at the loading and dumping stations. In the stables the lighting was also limited to an occasional carbide lamp. Consequently the mules soon became quite blind!

Blindness in the dark depths of the earth was not a serious

handicap. The mules memorized the location of their stalls. Mostly they trudged back and forth in the same drift day after day. Like the human blind, they learned their routes perfectly. They never bumped into the timbers or into the protruding rock walls as they made their rounds.

In the beginning they worked six days each week. Like the working elephants of Asia, they flatly refused to work on Sunday. Later, when the forty-hour week was adopted, they came to accept the extra day as their right. Again they refused to work except during regular working hours. (The writer experienced the same phenomenon with ranch mules. In an emergency, it was no problem to get horses to work on the Lord's day. But it took some language not recommended for the morning services to get the mules to forgo their day of rest!)

The mules received the best of care. They were fed only the top grades of hay and oats. A veterinarian checked on their physical condition once each week, and periodically a representative of the SPCA was lowered into the mine to inspect their living and working conditions. At the Empire Mine, at least, no complaint was ever registered.

As mentioned earlier, most deep mines of the world increase in temperature as the depth increases. The normal temperature gradient is about five degrees for each thousand feet. The Grass Valley mines were unique. There was no temperature change. Year around, and at every depth, the temperature remained at sixty-two degrees Fahrenheit. The mines were also "wet"; that is, there was always moisture on the rock walls. The relative humidity was therefore almost a hundred percent. In the slight chill and in the dampness, even the tough mules were subject to equine rheumatism and arthritis. In time they had to be retired.

Their size prohibited their being taken to the surface and turned out to pasture, so they were allowed the freedom of an underground paddock. There they were given the best of care until the swelling of their joints made it all too obvious that they were suffering. Then the veterinarian mercifully put them to sleep.

Now their bodies could be trussed tightly enough to allow

them to be fitted into the ore cars. At the surface they were given a decent burial.

The drivers, or "mule skinners," often became very attached to their charges. At the very least they now had someone, or something, to talk to as they made their dreary rounds through the darkened drifts. Most often after only a few round trips, the mule would know the route better than the driver, who could, and often would, take a nap in one of the cars as the mule made its way between the loading and the dumping stations.

The mule would stop at the exact spot for the loading or the dumping, and it knew by the sound when to move ahead to position the following car. If switches on the miniature railroad had to be thrown, the mule stopped at exactly the right spot to wait for the driver to awaken and work the proper lever.

Therein hangs the tale of one man and his mule.

Old Jim Crawford swore that his mule, Jerry, was so smart that he had taught himself to put his nose down to feel the switches as he approached. If they were set properly, he would continue on without stopping. Jim bragged that his mule was indeed so intelligent that he had reasoned that it was much easier to keep the cars rolling than to start them once more. Thus the nose trick.

Some of the miners put up $25 and called Jim's bluff. He never accepted the bet. He alibied by saying his mule was so self-conscious that he got embarrassed when strangers were around and would not perform.

It was a fact, however, that Jerry was so smart and so well trained that Jim's mule-driving job was in effect a form of early retirement after he became too arthritic to do more timbering in the mine.

In return, Jim saw that Jerry got the freshest oats and the greenest hay. He also made sure that the stable man cleaned his mule's stall each day and provided it with plenty of fresh bedding straw. Jerry's smartness was not all put to Jim's advantage. The mule had larceny bred in his blood. He refused to go back to work after the lunch break until Jim cut off a sizeable chunk of his plug chewing tobacco for his blackmailing friend. Jerry did not chew the aromatic gummy mixture of pungent leaves and molasses. He ate it!

As to all, the end must come. Old Jerry had been retired in the underground corral only a few months when it became obvious that he could no longer stand except with great pain. He must not be allowed to suffer longer.

Even the tough old miner cried unabashedly when he asked the "vet" to put his old friend out of his misery. Tears streamed down his time-worn face as he held the head of his companion of the drifts in his arms while the doctor administered the lethal potion.

Knowing Jim's intentions, however, one must surmise that, although he did love that old mule, his showing of grief was not entirely sincere!

Jim had worked at a menial job all his life, but he was not dumb. He realized that he too must retire someday soon. On the meager wage of the mine he had not been able to save for his old age. There was no pension, and Social Security had not as yet been dreamed of. Old people were supposed to live with their children. That was the main reason for having such large families. At least one of the offspring would be grateful enough to care for his helpless parents.

Unfortunately, Jim had never married. He was almost sure that he did have sons working in the mines, but they were known by different names. They never suspected that the sly old bachelor might be their biological father. Anyway, Jim knew that he must make some provision for his old age. If he did not, he would soon find himself a guest of the county poor farm. He also knew that one trip from the farm to the county hospital was all that was allowed. Shortly after the beginning of the second hospitalization, the patient was given his medicine from the "black bottle." It was surprising how the cost of caring for the aged could be reduced by the judicious use of a bit too much of that medicine, which, at first, made the sick feel so good!

Before becoming a mule skinner, Jim, as did all underground workers, kept a keen and practiced eye opened for the glint of gold in the stopes (areas where the ledges were being worked from below). If gold was visible to the naked eye, the ore was worth investigating, and most probably it would be worth highgrading (stealing).

One day while setting timbers to support the hanging wall of a stope, which was known to produce highgrade ore, Jim's hammer struck and dislodged a piece of the ledge quartz. Instead of falling, the broken rock was held suspended by several strands of gold!

Jim immediately sent his helpers for some timbers cut to exact dimensions. Once alone, he used a bar and a pick to break out about a hundred pounds of the ore. To his amazement, and to his delight, almost half of the quartz proved to be "picture rock" (studded with gold and bright enough to be cut into jewelry). He put the treasure in a powder box and buried it at the side of the drift below. He was busy wedging a stull in place when his helper returned.

Jim was not rich yet. He still had a problem. How to get the highgrade out of the mine and into the hands of an illicit gold buyer? He could smuggle out a small piece at a time, but observation had taught him that sooner or later he would be caught. If sooner, he would not be allowed to reenter the mine. His treasure would be lost. He bided his time.

When he was relieved of the back-breaking job of timbering, he moved the treasure box to a spot near the stable. Periodically he was able to add more pieces of rich ore to the cache. He used two methods to accomplish this. First, he habitually examined every piece of quartz on the top of the cars that showed any prospect of carrying gold. Occasionally he found a piece rich enough to bury. He also bought a few pieces of particularly rich rock from miners who had access to rich ledges but had no means of getting their finds out of the mine. He paid about twenty cents on the dollar and added his investment to the other highgrade. The miners asked no questions.

When Jerry was put to sleep, Jim gave the stable man $2 to take the rest of his shift off. Go get drunk if he wanted, but get the hell out of there, he wanted to be alone! He would feed the rest of the mules and clean the stable. He also would fix up the dead mule's body so that it could be sent up the next morning for burial.

Alone, Jim produced a razor-sharp knife and proceeded to do a quick autopsy. Only he did not need to examine the organs and diagnose. With the mule laid open, a quick slash of the knife allowed the content of the stomach to spill out and mix with the manure on the stable floor. It was replaced with the highgrade from the buried powder box.

The sewing job need not be neat. The poor old mule's legs were trussed fore and aft, and secured by lengths of used steel cable. Jim took no chances of having a rope break, or of its being cut, exposing the crude bit of surgery.

Jim took the next day off. Oh, he reported for work, but once he reached the stable, grief overcame him. He was too stricken to work. Instead he watched the body of his mule begin its journey to the top; then he followed on the next "man skip." On the surface he marched slowly behind the burial party to the mule cemetery and carefully marked the exact location of the grave.

At midnight, three days later, he started a little job of grave robbery. Fate nearly denied him the enjoyment of his stolen treasure. He was almost killed by a couple of muckers. A mule had dropped dead in a drift near where they had been working. They were prepared for just such an opportunity. They had some fifty pounds of highgrade, which they had broken into quarter-to half-inch pieces. This they mixed with several gallons of water. They forced a three foot length of garden hose down the dead beast's throat, put a funnel on the exposed end, and poured the mixture of rock, gold, and water into the mule's stomach. The veterinarian reasoned that the mule's bloated condition accounted for the heart attack. He did not investigate further.

Jim was throwing the last shovel of dirt from above Jerry's slightly decomposed body when the muckers arrived. They jumped into the opened grave and worked Jim over with pick handles. Just before a lethal blow was struck, Jim managed to get through to the muckers that their mule was "next door."

Jim was hospitalized for several days. He claimed that he had been picked up staggering along the Colfax road. He said that he had been thrown from a friend's Model T when it jackknifed into a ditch.

A few days after his release from the hospital, Jim exhumed his treasure from its most recent burial plot. The original cache had grown until it contained almost a hundred and fifty pounds of quartz and gold. He crushed it and panned it. In all, he got nearly a thousand ounces of the precious metal—a small fortune for a man in his circumstances.

When the city doctors said that Jim's injuries had permanently disabled him, his friend's automobile insurance paid off handsomely. Old Dr. Jones at the local hospital shook his head. He knew that the injuries had not been that serious. But he said nothing. After all, it was only insurance company money!

"There goes Muley Jim," the off-shift miners said once each year as they watched Jim make his way slowly to the mule cemetery on the ridge between the Empire and the Orleans mines.

Jim had the last laugh. Let them think he was a little "touched in the head" from the "auto accident." After all, he could well afford the bunch of storebought flowers he placed on the grave of his best friend and benefactor.

One story that Mike liked to tell during the last few years of his life was that of the highgrading that never took place. For obvious reasons he could tell the story only to close relatives and intimate friends.

Mike was so unfortunate during the last few years of his life as to develop a rectal cancer. Fortunately, the malignancy was discovered in time. An operation was performed that removed the diseased tissues. The infection did not spread, but Mike was most distraught. The surgeon had to rebuild the outlet of the intestinal tract. Thereafter, Mike was force to live with a colostomy.

Mike cursed the lot that fate had dealt to him, but actually he took the situation in stride. He had only one real lament. As he told the listener of all the schemes used by the miners and mill men to get gold away from the mine, including the concealment of small bits in body cavities, he would say, "Hell, if I could just have had this convenient opening in my side while I was working in the mines, I'd have been the richest man in Grass Valley!"

He left the exact process to the imagination of the listener. Of course everyone knew that he was not serious. He always lived by the "rule." And anyone who did not was a "dirty SOB!"

Although he never engaged in any large-scale highgrading, the reputation he carried was often an inconvenience. When he did make a little extra money by some activity, or by a fortunate investment, he was unable to spend it. Spending money from an unknown source often led to a miner's being laid off by the mine where he was working. No reason was given, and with no union representation, none needed to be given.

During the time when he still had to have steady employment in the mines, Mike found a small pocket on the bedrock on the McGuire Ranch while he was looking for the lost lead. This was long after the placer gold was supposed to have been worked out. He had no trouble getting cash for the gold, but he was at a loss as to what to do with the money. No one would believe that he had not highgraded it from the Empire, where he was then working.

He wanted to buy a house in town, so he resorted to subterfuge. He approached George Starr, the superintendent and general manager of the Empire. He told Starr that he wanted to buy the house on Richardson Street, which he was now renting. The price was $2,500. He had only $500 at the moment, but the owner demanded all cash. Would he make him a loan of $2,000?

Starr knew Mike very well. After all they were neighbors, and while they did not move in the same social set, they were as friendly as a mine manager and a hard-rock miner could be.

Starr knew that Mike was good for the money and that he would pay eventually. He also knew that, barring the sale of the ranch land, Mike's pay was not sufficient to justify a loan of that amount. Repayment would mean real sacrifice. Should something go wrong Mike would be tempted to take a little more than the usual miner's share to keep up the payments. But, of more importance, if he loaned money to one, a hundred others would be coming into his office asking for the same kind of treatment. He could not set the precedent.

"No, Mike," he said, "I just don't have the money right now."

Mike showed great disappointment. "Mr. Starr," he said, "you and I have been neighbors and friends all these years. I thought sure that I could depend on you when I really needed the money."

Then he applied a little pressure: "You know, Mr. Starr, Tom and Jim and Minnie have been after me to find out just how close the Empire is working to the McGuire line! So far I've held them off. I've told them to forget it and not to spend any money on an underground survey."

Starr had to do some fast thinking. The last thing in the world he wanted was for Tom to get underground in his mine with transit and a steel tape. Although he would not do so intentionally, his men might go too far in following a highgrade lead.

"Mike, I've got an idea," he said. "Why don't you write to Jim? I hear that he is doing real well in South Africa. You can put up your share of the ranch as security until you can pay him back. That will solve your problems."

Mike could hardly keep a straight face. "Why, thank you, Mr. Starr. Now why didn't I think of that? Sure, Jim will let me have the money!"

Mike laughed all the way to town. Had Starr not thought of the suggestion, he was all set to think it up on the spot. Now he was off the hook. He had an explanation for his sudden affluence.

Even in death Mike and Lucy were not allowed to rest undisturbed in the red soil of the Sierra foothills.

The original McGuire plot in the Catholic cemetery in Grass Valley would receive no more after Jim was interred. Mike purchased other space for the remaining direct decendants of the original pioneer family and their spouses.

He chose a spot under a majestic oak where he and Birdie, and Lucy and Otto might rest, there to be away from the pressures of living in a world so changed from the simple people and the simple pleasures of their youth—away from the rustic society they had known and loved so well.

That particular spot was chosen, not only because the oak would provide shade for the visitors who must come to pay their respects, but because it occupied the crest of a ridge from where the forested slopes of Osborn Hill, and the pine-and cedar-shaded glades of "McGuire Flat," stood green and inviting across the valley of Wolf Creek. From the chosen spot could be seen the weathered head frames of the Idaho-Maryland, the North Star, and the Empire Mines, by those visitors who understood and were saddened by nostalgia for the mining days.

Just a month before Birdie was destined to join the others in the "long sleep," the Diocese dictated that an access road be cut through to a new area of "God's Acres." The remains would have to be moved to make way for "progress."

Today, if one cares to listen to the whispering of the Sierra breezes in the branches of the oaks and of the evergreens, one can hear Lucy lament, "They always picked on me! No one could ever leave me alone!"

Or when the storms of winter bend the stately trunks and whip the fragile branches of these same trees, the voice of the youngest of the Irish clan, the McGuires of Grass Valley, touched with just the faintest of Irish brogue, comes through loud and clear.

Mike was never one to mince words. To those who can hear, he damns the idiots who laid out the cemetery in the first place: "If only the Irish had been allowed to manage things! But what was to be expected of the Italians, of the Spanish, and especially of the few Cousin Jacks who had joined the 'true church'?"

If the listener can hear, he can also imagine Mike shouldering his way through the "Heavenly Host," bent on reaching the side of Saint Patrick. Once there he would gain the ear of the Saint, and the Saint would listen. How could he refuse? That the petitioner was a true son of Ireland was written on his face. His every expression and his every spoken word set him aside as one who, figuratively at least, had kissed the Blarney Stone.

The patron saint of all the Irish would establish order once more in the gold country. Why, he might use his saintly authority to order that the Tommyknockers refill the empty stopes in the deep recesses of the famous mines with gold-specked quartz! Then the earth would spew forth its riches once again. Then the Irish miners would be rewarded for having faith that God would take care of his own.

Who knows? They might allow the Cousin Jacks to work the rich stopes once more. Most certainly, with a sly wink, they would overlook the extra weight of the "highgrade" in the miners' dinner buckets, as they came off shift.